If you're interested in department store history, buy his books.
—*David Sullivan,* Philadelphia Inquirer

[Hutzler's] *is beautifully written obviously by someone who has an affinity for department stores.*
—*Frederick N. Rasmussen,* Baltimore Sun

[Wanamaker's is] *a loving history of the store that once "defined Center City Philadelphia."*
—*Ronnie Polaneczky,* Philadelphia Daily News

[Gimbels] *is a passionate history of an iconic store.*
—*Jim Higgins,* Milwaukee Journal Sentinel

Lisicky recalls the glory days of Gimbels [with] an evocative book.
—*Marylynn Pitz,* Pittsburgh Post-Gazette

Retail fans can now take a stroll down memory lane with Lisicky, a department store historian.
—*Jan Gardner,* Boston Globe

Baltimore's Bygone Department Stores: Many Happy Returns *is a follow-up to Lisicky's wildly popular Hutzler's book…* [but this book] *widens the scope to look at other iconic stores* [that] *captured the cash* and *the imaginations of Baltimoreans.*
—Baltimore Magazine

To hear Mr Lisicky talk, writing [Hutzler's] *was simply his destiny.*
—*Alan Feiler,* Baltimore Jewish Times

WOODWARD & LOTHROP

A Store Worthy of the Nation's Capital

MICHAEL J. LISICKY

INTRODUCTION BY TIM GUNN

Charleston   London

THE
History
PRESS

Published by The History Press
Charleston, SC 29403
www.historypress.net

First published 2013

Manufactured in the United States

ISBN 978.1.62619.060.3

Library of Congress CIP data applied for.

To my friend John, who is just as much of a Washington institution as Hot Shoppes, Hechinger and Hahn Shoes.

And to our dear family friend Claire, who is perhaps the most fervent supporter of my "little books."

Contents

Preface

I am almost as fond of the American car industry as I am of the American department store industry. I especially love those great stylish cars that General Motors built between the 1950s and the 1970s. Every one of the five General Motors divisions catered to a different clientele, and each division offered a certain type or strength of car. I find it easy to equate Washington's former department store market with those great General Motors automobiles. I see Woodward & Lothrop as the Buick of Washington. A strong car that was better than it needed to be and offered more perks than most cars. A Buick Riviera was a sign of strength and class. It was a car that you were proud to drive and be seen driving. The Hecht Company was Washington's Chevrolet. Hecht's offered solid merchandise that was priced for most budgets, just like a Chevrolet. Millions of Americans packed their families into Chevrolet station wagons that were solid and dependable. You could drive a standard Bel Air or a sporty Impala. Just like Chevrolet, Hecht's offered a wide variety of options. Garfinckels was the Cadillac of Washington. Only certain people could afford Cadillacs, and only certain people could afford Garfinckels. Some Washingtonians were not even allowed to shop at Garfinckels. Garfinckels wasn't the department store that Woodward & Lothrop and the Hecht Company were. It did not offer every possible type of merchandise. You couldn't buy a blender at Garfinckels, but it suited its regular, high-income, loyal clientele just fine. It was a status symbol to own something from Garfinckels, just like it was a status symbol to own an Eldorado. You didn't need to own a car as exclusive as an Eldorado,

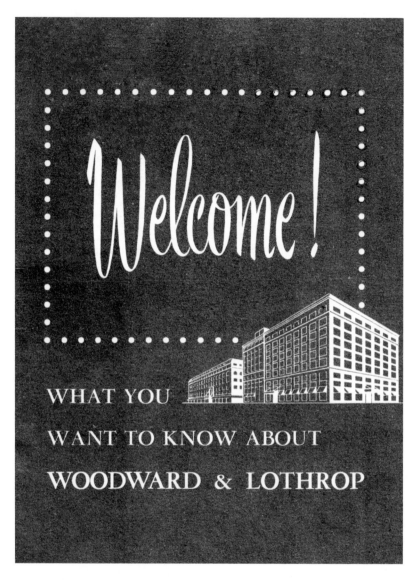

A cover of an employee manual from the early 1950s shows Woodies' Main Store and its recently acquired North Building. *Collection of the author.*

but a number of people aspired to drive one. Lansburgh's and Kann's never fit the General Motors mold, but perhaps both stores were the Ramblers of Washington. The Rambler was a good basic car that suffered from a lackluster image. Like the Rambler, Lansburgh's and Kann's struggled to make it into the 1970s and eventually disappeared. Unfortunately, a changing customer who wanted more car for less money challenged the American car industry just as competition from discounters and out-of-town retailers killed local department stores. Lower prices and expanded offerings won out over retail loyalty, and Washington's department stores suffered no differently than those in other American cities.

I was never exactly comfortable referring to Woodward & Lothrop as "Woodies." I grew up in the Philadelphia area, where we had our own iconic retailing institutions. In my family's 1960s-era traditional suburban household, it would have seemed blasphemous to call Strawbridge & Clothier "Strawbridge's" or Lit Brothers "Lits." My father still refers to Sears as Sears, Roebuck, and I recently found cancelled checks from 1967 that my mother made out to "the Great Atlantic & Pacific Tea Co." Whenever I visited Washington, I thought that it was disrespectful to call the store anything but Woodward & Lothrop, until I learned most Washingtonians affectionately called the store "Woodies."

A nickname is an endearing term usually given to a friend, and many people saw Woodward & Lothrop as their friend. The flagship store was located smack in the heart of downtown Washington and equidistant from all of Washington's other big stores. The store was an industry leader in a city that didn't have a large industrial component. By the early 1950s, this "one-price house" became a retailing behemoth, employing over five thousand people. A corporate annual report from 1952 stated, "Woodward & Lothrop is an institution of individuals dedicated to providing better merchandise and rendering better service for the people of the Washington area." Perhaps the key word in that statement is the word "better." Woodward & Lothrop never strived to be the best but certainly never found itself at the bottom. The store was famous for being better and became a store where you wanted to shop, not a store where you had to shop.

In 1955, Woodward & Lothrop published a commemorative book entitled *From Founders to Grandsons* in celebration of the company's seventy-fifth anniversary. It is a wonderful documentation of the growth of this important institution. Creatively narrated as a personal story, *From Founders to Grandsons* documents the company's earlier years extremely well. I did not, and could not, rewrite that 1955 publication. Besides, that book only covers seventy-five years, and Woodward & Lothrop continued in business for another forty. One of the chapters in *From Founders to Grandsons* is entitled "May It Last Forever." It was the motto given to the store's Twenty Year Club that honored store members for their years of longtime service. Unfortunately the great iconic department store did not last forever, and it finally succumbed to changing ownership and stiff competition in 1995. I feel that it is my mission to tell the entire story of "the Store Worthy of the Nation's Capital." I am convinced that Washingtonians and department store fanatics absolutely do care about Woodward & Lothrop. And perhaps one day, I will be comfortable calling the place "Woodies."

Acknowledgements

I would like to thank the following people who remember and learn about a store "Worthy of the Nation's Capital": Tim Gunn, for his personal and engaging introduction about his earlier days in the business and for being just as nice and genuine in person as he is on television; Jan Whitaker, for her tea room essay, friendship and inspiration; Georgetown University professor Richard Longstreth, for the access to his amazing image collection—his books on retail history and architecture are comprehensive and impressive; and to members of the Woodward and Lothrop families, including Brainard Parker, Nathaniel Orme and Nancy Luttrell Orme. Thank you for allowing me a chance to peak into a retail dynasty.

Special thanks go to two incredible institutions: the Historical Society of Washington, D.C., and the Washingtoniana Department at the Martin Luther King Jr. Free Public Library. Thank you Anne McDonough at the Historical Society's Kiplinger Research Library, the home of the Woodward & Lothrop company records and Faye Haskins and Michele Casto at the Main Library's Washingtoniana Department, the home of the photographic archives of the defunct *Washington Star* newspaper and various vertical files containing corporate papers, news articles and ephemera.

A thank-you goes also to several prominent "Woodlothians" who shared their personal stories and helped personalize this book: Ed Hoffman, Robert Mang, the amazing Waldo Burnside, Robert Mulligan, Donald Godfrey, David Mullen, Howard Lehrer, Robbie Snow and Shirley Mihursky. Additional thanks go to Washingtonians John DeFerrari, John Findley and

Sally Rosen. I must also acknowledge the support and encouragement from my friends at the Baltimore Symphony Orchestra, including Phil Munds, Madeline Adkins, Sharon Myer and Katherine Needleman.

Once again, my heart breaks for my long-suffering wife, Sandy, who has spent large parts of her busy life working to make my six books readable and respectable, and for my fourteen-year-old daughter, Jordan, who must always be wondering if this department store madness will ever end.

Introduction

Woodward & Lothrop was my closet. I had nice clothes as a kid and as a teen because Woodies' merchandise was relevant and affordable. Woodies was the barometric gauge of how people in Washington wanted to dress. You went to Hecht's for appliances, dishwashers, sporting goods and casual clothing. Garfinckel's was where you went for great gifts. There was just something so glamorous about shopping at Garfinckel's. But most of us in Washington shopped at Woodies.

My grandmother once told us about a wedding that she had attended and how lovely it was. She told us that she said something about "Senator Trivet." My grandmother was a very politically minded lady, but my mother and sister were confused. "Senator Trivet? From where?" "From Woodies!" she answered. We later learned that she had been referring to her wedding gift to the bride—she "sent her a trivet" from Woodies.

I never saw my grandmother without a hat. She was just one of those ladies. I remember taking her to Seven Corners because it had a Lord & Taylor. We would eat at the store's Bird Cage restaurant, and she knew the store manager, Mr. Green, very well. One day, my grandmother went to Lord & Taylor and took back a pair of shoes because the heels had worn down. I remember asking her, "Well that's terrible. How long have you had them?" She said, "Three years." But they took them back, no questions asked. They were very gracious.

There was a Saks on the Washington border near Maryland, but my mother and grandmother never shopped there. They were extremely opposed to New York. Washington is more conservative; it is more important to blend in than to show off. More likely than not, we went to Garfinckel's in Spring Valley.

My first job was at the Hecht Company. I had just graduated school, and I was a sales associate in the art supplies department. I went through basic training, and they told me that I was the only person who ever scored a 100 on the customer service tests. One of the store's rules was, "Under no circumstances do you ever smell the armpits" of a returned item. You didn't ask any questions as long as there wasn't a stain on it. My first day was a Saturday, and the department manager called in sick. The other sales associate also called in sick, and I was all alone. I had never worked the floor before, even though I had all this training. The place was mobbed. And it was the olden days, so nothing was computerized. When people paid with checks, I accidentally put their check numbers in as "cash received." The machine kept telling me that I owed the wrong amount of change. If there were items that didn't have a price on them, I'd ask, "How much would you like to pay for it?" I didn't want to inconvenience anyone, and I had been told that "the customer is always right." The day's accounting was all screwed up, and it was all because of me. I left behind a real mess. The next day, I came in to work, and after about an hour with the manager, they fired me. It didn't matter that I scored a 100; I was the worst.

I left Washington in 1983. At that point, there weren't a lot of places to go downtown, and it was considered dangerous. You only went there because you worked there. But now, you wouldn't even know that it had been an unsafe neighborhood.

One thing that you can't discount is the whole culture of sales in this nation, where everybody thinks that if they just wait another day or two, the item will be cheaper. Regrettably, they're correct. That has had such a negative effect on the whole retail environment because that is how we think. In Europe, there are sales twice a year, period.

In so many ways, the shopping experiences at these department stores are really inextricable from my memories of childhood. You had to go to a store to buy anything. The stores didn't pretend to be something that they weren't. I never dreamed that these stores would go away. They were too much a part of our culture. Garfinckel's was the first to close. And then it was Woodies. That was too much change for my mother. She left town and moved to the beach.

TIM GUNN

Raised in Washington's Cleveland Park community, Tim Gunn is an American fashion icon and television personality. Since 2004, he has served as a fashion mentor on the television reality program Project Runway. In 1983, Tim Gunn left Washington to join the staff of the Parsons School for Design in New York City. He is a former faculty member at the Corcoran College of Art and Design and operated a sculpture studio in Washington's Dupont Circle neighborhood.

Boston Store

S amuel Walter Woodward and Alvin Mason Lothrop built and developed
a Washington retail institution, but their roots stemmed far from the
capital city. The men began their association as clerks at the Cushing &
Ames dry goods store on Boston's Hanover Street. Samuel was in charge of
dress goods and silks; Walter was the head of cloaks and shawls. Both men
were "of good New England ancestry" and had developed an interest in
creating an establishment that eliminated bargaining in favor of a one-price
system with the promise of satisfaction guaranteed.[1]

In 1848, Samuel Woodward was born in Damariscotta, Maine, near
the state's central coastline. At an early age, Woodward realized that his
employment options were limited along Maine's coast. By the time he
reached eighteen years old, Samuel Walter Woodward—or Walter, as his
friends and colleagues called him—left Maine for Boston and became a clerk
at the Shepard Brothers dry goods store. Friends called Walter "a practical
man of action with a keen sense of ambition."

Alvin Lothrop hailed from South Acton, Massachusetts, located
about twenty miles northwest of Boston. Lothrop's family roots traced
back to the Revolutionary War, and some of his ancestors fought in the
battle at Concord. Born in 1847, he received his early retail training
at the Tuttle, Jones and Wetherbee Country Store in his hometown.
But like Woodward, Alvin Lothrop knew that success did not lie
near his family's home, and he moved to Boston for employment and
financial opportunities.

Pioneers . . .

SAMUEL WALTER WOODWARD   ALVIN MASON LOTHROP

Two portraits of store founders Samuel Walter Woodward and Alvin Mason Lothrop after they arrived in Washington from the Boston area. These photographs were featured in an edition of the store's *Woodlothian* magazine. *Collection of the author.*

Both men came to Boston's Cushing and Ames store in 1870 but grew disenchanted with the company's business practices. Like many retail operations at the time, Cushing and Ames ordered their salesmen to haggle with customers to determine the right price for merchandise. When a price could not be agreed on, employees often chased the lost customers out of the store's doors.[2] Cushing and Ames did not allow customers to return merchandise once the transaction was completed. Walter and Alvin disagreed with the store's management. This disagreement came to a head over the sale of a shawl. Even as shawls were growing out of fashion, Cushing and Ames refused to reduce the price of a shawl that had been in the company's stock for quite some time. Walter and Alvin urged that the shawl's price be reduced to "hasten its sale." Cushing and Ames held to the theory that "for every good shawl, there is a good woman to buy it." Walter and Alvin disagreed with this sales philosophy and felt that there was not a future for them at Cushing and Ames. After three years, the two men left and opened their own business.

In 1873, Woodward and Lothrop purchased a small store in Chelsea, Massachusetts, called "the Button Shop." The store was owned by Billy McCoy, "the Button Boy." McCoy creatively used poetry within his button shop advertisements, but his store was not a commercial success:

> *Billy McCoy, the Button Boy,*
> *is not of buttons made,*

But when you see, both you and he,
you'll make a button trade.[3]

Walter and Alvin were not interested in selling buttons, but the store was in
an ideal location. The store, situated at 222 Broadway in Chelsea's Pythian
Hall, incorporated all their revolutionary business practices. They worked
long hours and never kept their eyes off the local competition in Chelsea
and nearby Boston. The Chelsea store was successful, but Walter and Alvin
wanted to expand and find a new location in a new city. Their ideas and
ambitions expanded farther than the town of Chelsea. Walter boarded a
train bound for Omaha and made regular stops to survey the local markets.

Walter's first stop was in New York, where a friend who worked at the iconic
A.T. Stewart & Co. store encouraged him to travel south instead of west.
"Go South, Walter, if you want a good opening. Baltimore and Washington
are both waiting for a good store," his friend advised.[4] Before traveling to
Omaha, Walter visited Baltimore and enjoyed its familiar resemblance to
Boston. He continued to Washington and was impressed with what he saw.
The book *From Founders to Grandsons* stated that Walter was captivated by the
nation's Capital.

Walter was pleased with Baltimore, but Washington was an entirely new
world. Here stood the staunch stone guardians of the Republic, the broad,
tree-lined avenues thronged with carriages—a city of the future set in the
eastern horizon of nineteenth-century America.

Walter Woodward continued on his planned train ride and scouted
locations in a variety of Midwest towns, including Kansas City, Missouri;
Atchison, Kansas; and, his final destination, Omaha, Nebraska. None of
the midwestern towns excited Walter more than Washington. He realized
that Washington was an important city still in its infancy, and it offered plenty
of opportunities for a one-price store. Walter wired his observations to Alvin
in Chelsea, and the two men soon relocated their business to Washington,
D.C. Brainard Parker, one of Walter Woodward's great-grandsons, states
that both Woodward and Lothrop were smart and savvy businessmen. "Both
founders had a pretty strong work ethic. They knew that their fortunes would
be better made in the District," says Parker. "They were obviously talented,
dedicated, and hard working people."

"Alvin, This Is the Place for Us"

The true merchant is more than a mere distributor of goods. Vision plays a large part in the success of every successful one, and this quality characterized these two men.[5]
—*William Knowles Cooper*
General secretary of the Washington YMCA
1908–1929

Mr. Woodward and Mr. Lothrop had an unwavering faith in Washington. In their vision, they saw a city constantly enlarging its population, rebuilding its structures and becoming more and more the center of the best life in the nation.

On February 25, 1880, Woodward and Lothrop opened the "Boston Dry Goods House" at 75 Market Space in downtown Washington. One of the building's greatest features was a prominent sign that read "One Price." The opening day's advertisement in the *Washington Post* begged the ladies of Washington and the vicinity to examine its collection of silks, linens and muslins that were freely shown with "no one importuned to purchase."[6] The formal name of the business was Woodward, Lothrop & Cochrane. Walter and Alvin convinced Charles E. Cochrane, an aspiring merchant, to invest in their revolutionary one-price business. The name "Boston House" helped cement the company's original roots to its new Washington customer base and implied a level of culture to its new customers. A number of unrelated department stores in cities such as Milwaukee, Erie, Providence, Ashville, Wilkes-Barre and many others operated under the name "Boston Store." Woodward, Lothrop &

Cochrane's Boston House, also referred to as the Boston Store, rapidly grew in sales and size.

Woodward, Lothrop & Cochrane established its new business as "an institution of individuals dedicated to providing better merchandise and rendering better service to the people of the Washington area." The three men acquired 79 Market Space, and the store grew to thirty-one departments of first-class dry goods and millinery. Many historians credit the Boston House as Washington's first department store. When the partners were unable to acquire the storefront between their two neighboring operations, they found the store a "new, elegant and spacious premises" at 921 Pennsylvania Avenue. On December 4, 1880, this new, larger Boston House opened its doors. Many of the store's competitors predicted that the business would collapse after a few months because of the potential low profit margin of a one-price-for-all concept. The Boston House brought not only a revolutionary pricing concept to Washington but also elegant show windows to the developing city. On opening day, the Boston House displayed bright summer clothing and bathing suits in its front windows during a major snowstorm. Critics scoffed at this unusual form of advertising, but it boldly captured the public's attention. A large investment of promotions and advertising became a hallmark for the company for many decades.

Within a few months, Walter and Alvin were at odds with Charles Cochrane over the handling of the business. The disagreement was irreparable, and Walter and Alvin purchased Charles's share of the store at great personal financial sacrifice.[7] In April 1881, Charles opened his own "one price cash principle" store at New York Avenue and Fifteenth Street called Cochrane & Co. The store featured linens, white goods and laces. No record exists of Cochrane & Co. operating beyond 1881. The Boston House persevered with annual sales of $180,000 and two hundred employees working throughout the business's three selling floors. Walter Woodward managed the store's merchandising, and Alvin Lothrop supervised the company's physical operations and customer relations. An editorial in the *Washington Star* newspaper from January 20, 1941, stated:

> *So carefully was their merchandise chosen, so determined was their insistence upon quality, so thorough was their training of salespeople that even though the* [one-price, return if not satisfactory] *policy was then so revolutionary, they knew that it was in the interest of the consumer.*

The store operated with the policy of "quality first and price second, courtesy to every customer, rich or poor...and the return of each [item] was welcomed."[8] During its first few years of operation, the company did not net any profits. Once the business and its high sales volume were firmly established, Woodward & Lothrop enjoyed amazing growth in sales and reputation.

One piece of company folklore occurred at the Pennsylvania Avenue location. Soon after its grand opening, three Indians, all in feathers and paint, came to Washington and visited the store. The three men boarded the store elevator but either the weight limit was exceeded or the porter on the main floor confused his signals. The elevator subsided to the basement instead of elevating to the second floor. When the basement elevator opened, "the basement porter looked up and saw the Indians. One look was enough. He was out of the building and [did not return] again for hours."

When the two businessmen worked together at Cushing and Ames in Boston, they complained about the owners' reluctance to lower the price of unsold merchandise. In March 1885, Walter and Alvin instituted a new sale called "Remnant Day." Remnant Day was held on selected Fridays and offered dramatically lowered prices on unsold quality merchandise. Unlike the company's standards selections, items purchased as part of the Remnant Day sale were not available for return. The promotion worked, and Remnant Day became a company tradition well into the 1950s. The sale created more room at the store's Pennsylvania Avenue location, but even that could not accommodate the company's growth.

By 1886, the Boston House outgrew its Pennsylvania Avenue quarters and Walter and Alvin acquired property on the corner of Eleventh and F Streets NW. It was there, on April 2, 1887, that Woodward and Lothrop opened their doors as "the most complete [store] of its kind in this country and is unsurpassed by any similar establishment in the combination of architectural effect with light and convenient store rooms." Large crowds visited the store on opening day: "The crush was so great that according to another tradition, many of the feminine shoppers lost their bustles, which were later uncovered from under counters."[9] The Italian Renaissance structure, known as the Carlisle Building, was built for the company at the cost of $100,000. The five-story building contained elaborate projecting show windows, a grand staircase with carved cherry railings, writing desks with magazines and periodicals, a "Bureau of Information" desk to help answer random questions about the store and the city, a marble drinking fountain and two passenger elevators. The store was unlike anything that Washington had

This early image shows the Woodward & Lothrop stop at the intersection of Eleventh and F Streets NW. The photograph dates from circa 1915. *Courtesy of the Harris & Ewing Collection at the Library of Congress.*

ever seen before, but critics complained that its location outside of the city's centralized business district was located "practically in the wilderness."[10] This proved untrue as the company's annual sales ballooned to $867,000, and additional space was always needed. One of the other major changes at the new location was the company's name. It was now Woodward & Lothrop, with the tagline "Boston One-Price House" phased out in 1886.

Woodward & Lothrop sought growth not only at its Eleventh and F Street location but also at its newly opened branches in two neighboring cities. The company opened a branch store in Richmond, Virginia, in September 1891. The store, located at Broad and Adams Streets, specialized in staple goods. Woodward & Lothrop followed the Richmond store with a Baltimore location in 1893. Located at Park Avenue and Lexington Street in the heart of Baltimore's retail core, the store opened on March 15, 1893. The two men expressed hope and faith in the Baltimore venture because the city reminded them of their original Boston environs. The four-story store offered "high-class dry and fancy goods" that were available at "one-price only, qualities guaranteed at the best and the lowest prices, and money refunded upon request, giving the purchaser the benefit of any or all competition."[11] The company faced stiff competition in Richmond with Thalhimer Brothers and in Baltimore with Hutzler's and Joel Gutman & Company. Both Woodward & Lothrop locations were unsuccessful. The Richmond store closed in February 1893, even before the opening of the Baltimore location, and the Baltimore store closed within just a few months on December 30, 1893. The company cited the "shipping and communication difficulties" between its corporate headquarters and branch locations as reasons for the stores' failures. Woodward & Lothrop's success was in Washington, and the company focused all of its energy on its F Street store.

Woodward & Lothrop continued to grow its Washington business by purchasing adjacent properties along F Street. As each new storefront was acquired, the company broke through walls and installed archways so customers could easily travel from building to building. By 1897, Woodward & Lothrop was holding popular promotional events at the downtown store. The store's special events included pony rides, author lectures, darning machine demonstrations and art exhibitions. In December 1897, the store hosted a special collection of American Indian pottery, fabrics and paintings. A promotional advertisement announced, "It is seldom that we have a chance to become personally acquainted with the productions of the Indians, the privilege being generally confined to those able to visit the borders of their reservations."[12] And as the industry turned toward designer and ready-to-wear merchandise, Woodward & Lothrop opened a branch buying office in Paris in October 1900 at 43 Rue de Paradis. Washingtonian and fashion consultant Tim Gunn has strong feelings about the role Paris played in dictating fashion during the early part of the century:

> *I'm so woeful about everything going back to Paris. In terms of style, it regrettably does. It was a fashion incubator. Until World War II the United States was nothing but a nation of copiers. American manufacturers would go to all of the Paris shows, make sketches, and come back and copy everything.*
>
> *London was the hotbed of tailoring* [in the terms of men's clothing]…*Tailoring was the only area that* [another country] *eclipsed Paris in terms of fashion.*

Woodward & Lothrop followed the lead of other major American department stores with its display of exotic imports. The store offered "direct importations and American productions comprising exact styles as seen on the Boulevard, Bois de Boulogne, Champs Elysees of Paris and Hyde Park of London." Woodward & Lothrop strived to be "the most attractive and fashionable center in the National Capital."[13]

In April 1901, Woodward & Lothrop announced the purchase of the vacant St. Vincent's Orphan Asylum at Tenth and G Streets NW. Demolition and construction began immediately on an eight-story building that doubled the size of the company's existing operation. By the time construction was completed in 1904, the company's annual sales had reached almost $3 million. The store continued to promote elaborate window displays and vibrant interior decorations. Author Jan Whitaker recalls how holidays and anniversary displays helped enliven department store interiors. Whitaker comments on one Woodward & Lothrop display from Easter 1905: "The store went all-out for Easter, the culminating point of spring openings, and for decades second only to Christmas in sales. Purple and white bunting was wrapped around the pillars, and Japanese umbrellas and chariots made of

Women with parasols browse the windows at the downtown store around 1920. This image also shows the former Rich's shoe store corner location, adjacent to Woodies' downtown building. Rich's operated for 118 years, closing in 1987. *Courtesy of the National Photo Company Collection at the Library of Congress.*

large Easter eggs pulled by butterflies were suspended from a bamboo lattice hanging from the ceiling."[14]

Lothrop's health deteriorated during the last two years of his life, and "he could take no active part in the conduct of his business." He was confined to a wheelchair during his last few weeks, and on November 30, 1912, Alvin Mason Lothrop passed away after being stricken with apoplexy, a condition stemming from internal bleeding. Woodward & Lothrop closed its doors until after the funeral, where crowds of friends and business associates gathered to pay their respects. The Reverend Dr. Samuel H. Woodrow, pastor of the First Congregational Church, gave the eulogy. Woodrow remarked:

> *A broad-minded, whole-souled, sunny-hearted man has been taken from his earthly labors to his heavenly reward. It is not easy to fill his place in the business, philanthropic, or church life of the city, and it is still harder to fill his place in the hearts of many who knew or loved him.*[15]

Another eulogy appeared on November 30, 1912, in the *Washington Star* newspaper:

> *Alvin M. Lothrop came to Washington with his public spirited partner for a business location in 1880, and during the thirty-two years of his residence here he proved one of the most substantial factors in the development of the District. He was throughout his career a strict business man in his painstaking attention to his work, his constant endeavor to meet the needs of his trade, his prompt acceptance of opportunities offered for advancement. Mr. Lothrop held to a high standard of honor. He was always trustworthy, and, consequently, he was greatly trusted by his business associates and honored by all with whom he had relations.*

On the personal side, Mr. Lothrop was an exceptional man, warm in his affections, cordial in his friendships, heartily appreciative of the feelings of others and unfailingly devoted to the making of the ideal Washington.

One of Alvin Lothrop's grandchildren, Nancy Orme, recalls a family story regarding Alvin Lothrop. Orme says that her grandfather was a short man. "One day, an employee jumped on him and knocked him down. The employee thought that he was another kid but then [unfortunately] realized that he was the owner of the store," says Orme.

The department store continued to grow throughout the early 1900s. By 1913, the new F Street frontage was built and occupied. The store encompassed twelve acres of floorage, employed 1,500 Store Members and housed thirteen elevators, a roof garden and a café. But the company suffered another jolt when cofounder S. Walter Woodward died suddenly at his summer home in Stockbridge, Massachusetts, on August 1, 1917. The *Washington Post* stated, "Mr. Woodward's death was unexpected and caused deep sorrow to thousands of Washingtonians." Scores of colleagues in the public and private sector paid tribute to Walter at his funeral in Oak Hill Cemetery, and most city retail businesses closed their doors during the service out of respect for Woodward. Some of Walter's closest confidantes felt that the loss of his wife on June 5, "super induced by extreme heat," accelerated his passing.[16] One account of Walter Woodward's passing stated:

> *Representing a noted figure in commerce, church, and state—an educator and philanthropist—Mr. Woodward's name is indelibly recorded upon the records of the commercial, financial, educational, religious and civic organizations of city and country. A man whose strength of character was shown by his deeds, he was broad-minded, resourceful, enthusiastic, sincere in his convictions—a tower of strength amid his associates.*
>
> *Mr. Woodward's life was a well-balanced one, though his many activities left him but little opportunity for his own personal recreations. He loved the science of trade on which he attained such signal success and was happiest when employed in its undertaking. He helped to build an organization that will hold long his dominating influence and the principles upon which the firm was founded.*[17]

Woodward & Lothrop looked within its families for leadership after the passing of the two founders. The company declared that the store "would continue the business with the same sterling principles and high ideals that always governed the Founders, and it should be the steadfast purpose of all of us to do nothing that is in any way unworthy of the splendid Christian gentleman who founded this store." Walter's only son, Donald Woodward, succeeded his father. Donald assumed the presidency at age twenty-nine. He was one of the youngest presidents of a large American department store. Donald continued many of his father's philanthropic activities and continued to advance many employee welfare programs. Nathaniel Luttrell married Alvin Lothrop's only child, Harriet, and played an active role in the company. Harriet Luttrell passed away in 1919 when her daughter, Nancy, was only two years of age:

I was a little girl and I kept asking, "Where's my Mommy?" I was told that she had gone shopping. For a long time, all I wanted to do was to go down to Woodward & Lothrop and find her. I think it was a governess who told me. It was sort of mean. It wasn't right.

Nancy's brother, Alvin Lothrop Luttrell, became a driving, prominent force in the business in the later years. For several decades, Woodward and Lothrop family members continued to manage and expand the department store's operations.

In 1913, one of Walter's brothers, Fred Woodward, established the department store's Twenty Year Club. The Twenty Year Club "represents twenty years of achievement in an association of store members maintaining and contributing to a retail firm which is an institution in the community of Washington."[18] Every April, the club gathered for a special Good Fellowship Dinner. New members who had reached twenty years of service were inducted into the club. As part of the annual tradition, the new inductees participated in a musical production. For many years, the dinner was held in the Hotel Statler's Congressional Room, and new Twenty Year Club members received twenty-dollar checks and gift certificates. In 1956, Colonel John Tyssowski, Woodies' chairman of the board and son-in-law of founder Walter Woodward, discussed the Twenty Year Club with fellow members: "Some folks figure a job is just a job, what you get out of it is all that matters. I just hope someday these wrong-thinkers may have the good fortune to attend one of our Twenty Year Club get-togethers."[19]

As the business continued to grow and thrive, Woodward & Lothrop followed many of the retailing policies of other major stores, notably John Wanamaker in Philadelphia. Years later, Woodward & Lothrop and Wanamaker's formed a bond as the two retailers fought to retain market share in their respective cities. The founding Woodward, Lothrop and Wanamaker families had strong loyal ties to their individual churches; all families were very philanthropic in their communities, especially the Young Men's Christian Association, and Woodward and Wanamaker were early supporters of public education. Wanamaker had his own John Wanamaker Commercial Institute that educated boys and girls in academics and business practices, and Washington was home to the Woodward School for Boys. Both companies housed the city's largest bookstores, and both businesses were champions in bringing music into their stores. Wanamaker's was home to the world's largest pipe organ, and Woodward & Lothrop organized an employee chorus called the Woodlothians. During World War I, Woodward

& Lothrop employees gathered daily on the main floor and sang patriotic songs for fifteen minutes before the store opened. Other large Washington department stores engaged in "group sings" during the war. A *Washington Post* article praised Woodlothians and compared their usefulness and talent with the Wanamaker choruses in Philadelphia and New York. "There can be no doubt that the spirit of song helped win the war. Certainly it was a big factor in keeping up the courage and optimism of the people in the hours of darkness and days of danger," said the *Post*.[20] After the war, the other Washington stores ended their singing programs. The Woodlothian chorus continued for decades.

On April 15, 1921, Woodward & Lothrop opened its Down Stairs Store. The Down Stairs Store offered quality dependable merchandise. It was "a store within a store" and provided the same privilege of charge and delivery as the Main Store.

Similar to how Wanamaker broadcasted WOO in Philadelphia, Woodward & Lothrop was home to one of Washington's earliest radio stations, WIAY. The station broadcasted popular and classical music, as well as occasional shopping tips. WIAY went on the air in September 1922 but ceased broadcasting in July 1924.

The inventor of the slogan "The Customer is Always Right" is often credited to Philadelphia merchant John Wanamaker, although its true origin is frequently debated. Woodward & Lothrop abided by that retailing principle. Alvin Lothrop's granddaughter Nancy Orme says that that slogan was part of the store's success. "It meant a lot to the people who bought there," says Orme. By the early 1920s, Woodward & Lothrop was regarded as the largest department store in the country south of Philadelphia's Wanamaker's. In 1925, Woodward & Lothrop completed the first of two expansions that made it the biggest, best and most complete department store in Washington.

The Possible Years

W alter Woodward and Alvin Lothrop referred to the first seven years of their time in Washington as "the impossible years." As the two men introduced a one-price system along with customer satisfaction guarantees, they worked long hours, moving from storefront to storefront. Corporate history states, "those were the years Mr. Woodward and Mr. Lothrop amazed the business community of Washington by their seemingly impossible deeds." By the mid 1920s, Woodward & Lothrop was a solid institution. Department stores, such as Woodward & Lothrop, were massive emporiums that defined the character and culture of the cities they served. Their layouts were designed "to enhance the presentation of merchandise," and they "presented goods in an artful, theatrical, manner" so as to increase profile and sales.[21]

In 1925, Woodward & Lothrop embarked on a two-year expansion program. The middle portions of the store along Tenth and Eleventh Streets were rebuilt so that they matched the design of the F Street building. The final expansion of the block-square complex was completed on October 30, 1926. The original Carlisle building at Tenth and G Streets NW was replaced and the store enjoyed a consistent eight-story frontage on all four sides. "I can't think of another department store in this country that went to such great expense and presented a seamless exterior [over its many additions]," says architectural historian Richard Longstreth. One thousand employees formally celebrated the building's completion on Halloween Day 1926. Entertainment was provided by the Woodlothian Chorus and string

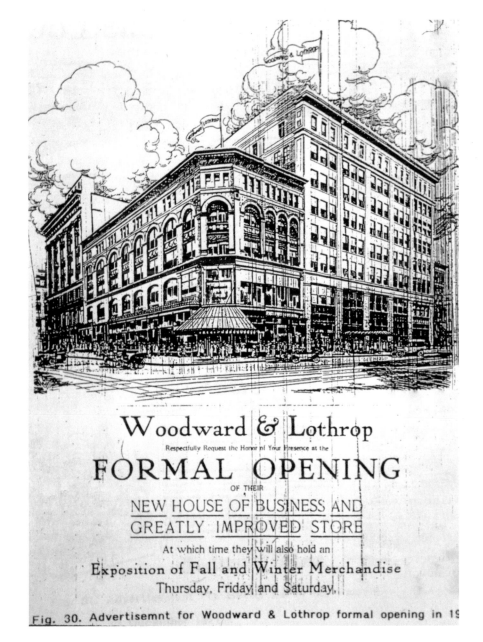

Fig. 30. Advertisemnt for Woodward & Lothrop formal opening in 19

Woodward & Lothrop announces the completion of an expansion dating from 1925.
Courtesy of the Richard Longstreth Collection.

orchestra and company officials declared that the expansion "carried a promise of even greater things" for the store's future. It was also a celebration of annual sales of $12,168,996.

The end of the decade brought economic hardship to the country, but Woodward & Lothrop survived the challenges. The Depression did not pack the solid punch in Washington that it did elsewhere in the country. "Washington is not a boom town," said orator William Everett. "We rarely feel the effects of boom conditions, and we just as rarely feel any major depression." The company's annual sales continued to grow as the Washington area enjoyed an average annual per capita income of $918, which was nearly double that of similarly sized cities. The federal government employed almost 28 percent of Washington-area residents, and that employment base helped the area maintain economic stability.

Woodward & Lothrop owed much of its success to good employee and community relations. This rapport existed well into later years. Former buyer Donald Godfrey says, "It was a pleasure to work for Woodward & Lothrop. I always said that I took good care of them, and they took good care of me." President Waldo Burnside credits the store's business practices:

> *The cornerstone of Woodward & Lothrop was satisfaction, good merchandise, good service and a good reputation. If a customer wanted to take something back, you had to do so without any questions. Sometimes you could tell that they weren't telling the truth, but you were told that "you were working with Woodies' money," and you took it back.*

Customer loyalty was strong. Former president Robert Mang adds, "Department stores were the first businesses to offer customer credit and credit adds a major source of loyalty." Former vice-chairman Robert Mulligan feels Woodward & Lothrop's success was linked to its community relations. "We were very active in town with our support of the National Symphony Orchestra, the Kennedy Center, and the Board of Trade. We developed loyalty through these sponsorships and with local charities. People knew us, and it gave us a good share of the market," says Mulligan.

In February 1930, Woodward & Lothrop celebrated its Golden Anniversary. The store was praised for fifty years of service based on "honesty and truthfulness."[22] The *Washington Post* declared, "The house of Woodward & Lothrop rests upon the solid foundation of character, which commands public confidence and insures prosperity." A company advertising brochure stated, "To be worthy of the nation's capital is no small accomplishment." In

Left: An advertisement in a Washington travel brochure touts Woodies' famous slogan alongside various interior photographs of the downtown store. *Collection of the author*.

Below: Woodward & Lothrop's book department celebrates the League of American Pen Women in the mid-1920s. *Courtesy of the National Photo Company Collection at the Library of Congress*.

only fifty years, Woodward & Lothrop had grown from a 1,700-square-foot storefront to a 500,000-square-foot emporium. The brochure continued:

> *The present store is recognized as one of the most modern and one of the most outstanding of the many fine department stores of the country. It must be, to serve a clientele whose discrimination is not surpassed by any in the world—a clientele that includes not only names that are distinguished in this country, but are of international repute.*

Company documents from 1930 stated:

> *With 50 years of public service, Woodward & Lothrop renews its pledge of unremitting perseverance; absolute justice for all at all times, in keeping pace with the city's growth in beauty and size, and the bending of every thought, effort and energy in making this store the representative institution of the Nation's Capital.*

In the 1930s, the store was seen as a small city within the greater city of Washington. Its layout was original as its merchandise was organized according to type and classification and its furniture department displayed its goods according to periods and ensembles. Customers could enjoy an ice cream confection in the basement Fountain Room, have a noon dinner in the store Tea Room and then return later in the day for afternoon tea. As the capital city grew, so did Woodward & Lothrop's needs. In 1937, the department store built a large Service Building on M Street NE. It was designed "loosely in the spirit of the modern classical public buildings then in vogue for federal projects."[23] The Service Building was just as large as the department store's main building and included stock rooms, receiving and marketing departments and a dry cleaning plant.

Woodward & Lothrop's seventh-floor Tea Room became a culinary destination in Washington. Shoppers ate alongside powerful businessmen and political dignitaries in the ornate surroundings. Most major American department stores contained at least one significant dining facility within their structures. Tearooms hosted special events such as fashion shows and organizational luncheons and kept shoppers in search of a meal from leaving the store. The Down Stairs Store was home to the Fountain Room, which offered "luncheon or refreshment while shopping." Some customers frequented the store's Tea Room weekly, or even daily. Former manager Shirley Mikursky remembers two such women:

TEA ROOM, SEVENTH FLOOR, MAIN STORE
WOODWARD & LOTHROP, WASHINGTON 13, D. C.

The Tea Room was a famous culinary and social destination that was located on the department store's seventh floor. *Collection of the author.*

There were these two little ladies who came and ate at the Tea Room every day. They were always dressed to the nines, but their hair always looked like birds' nests. You could usually find them in the elevator but they would be barking, bitching and moaning at each other. We called them "the Two Sisters."

The store also became known for its home furnishings department, which helped set it apart from Washington's other large retailers. Former president Robert Mang says that in later years the store had twenty-eight decorators on staff. The department store annually presented "Model Rooms" in its sixth-floor furniture department. Media Spokesperson Robbie Snow says that Model Room openings were always among the store's biggest events. "The designers designed a theme with vignettes, and the fashion department would present their new collections. It was a black tie event," says Snow. Woodward & Lothrop frequently presented and promoted designs and reproductions from Colonial Williamsburg. The longtime partnership with Colonial Williamsburg began in 1937. The sixth-floor Williamsburg Rooms presented furnishings that displayed the "18th century charm and urbanity,

Like many large American department stores, Woodward & Lothrop played an important role with the sales of war stamps and war bonds during World War II. *Collection of the author.*

which has captivated visitors to the Restoration at Williamsburg."[24] The collection was designed to promote grace and simplicity in Washington living rooms.

World War II presented challenges to American department stores. Workforces were greatly diminished as thousands of male employees were drafted into service. By 1941, Woodward & Lothrop actively recruited honorably discharged servicemen and women to help accommodate

Left: A rare image details the displays in the store's third-floor women's shoe department. *Collection of the author.*

Below: A postcard view showing the store's signature F Street store frontage. *Collection of the author.*

Employees and customers gather in the store's Downstairs Store to practice an air raid drill in the 1940s. *Courtesy of the D.C. Public Library, Washingtoniana Division.*

employee shortages. The company also lent its personnel to various U.S. government agencies on a dollar-a-year basis. There were merchandise shortages as well. Store promotions and annual events were cancelled out of respect for the war activities. As did many other large American stores, Woodward & Lothrop joined the war bond drive by setting up a "Victory Booth" on the store's main floor. The store asked shoppers to invest "10% of their salary and be 100% American." In March 1943, Woodward & Lothrop sold tickets for the captured two-man Japanese submarine on display in F Street's Capital Plaza. The tickets were only available to those who also purchased a war bond.

The economic structure of Washington remained relatively strong during the war. In 1943, the Washington market ranked number six in the country in retail sales. Unlike Baltimore, Philadelphia and Cleveland, Washington did not have a strong industrial employment engine. Rather, its economy was based on federal government jobs within the capital. The store was one of the region's largest private employers. "We weren't a part of the government, we were a business," says spokesperson Robbie Snow. As the war ended, the entire country enjoyed an era of economic prosperity. Once again, Woodward & Lothrop felt the need to grow, and it found its next opportunity right across G Street.

North Building

When Abram Lisner opened his new Palais Royal department store at the corner of Eleventh and G Streets NW, he stated, "Criticism of the new establishment is left to the public and the press. The buyers and their assistants await your verdict." The opening of the new building coincided with the opening of the new autumn fashion line. "According to annual custom the new season's goods are offered at nominal prices as souvenirs of the occasion."[25] The new Palais Royal was the first department store in Washington to be built from the ground up.

Lisner founded Palais Royal in 1877 at the corner of Twelfth Street and Pennsylvania Avenue. Pennsylvania Avenue was formerly a shopping district where shoppers chose to purchase goods from "stores that asked low prices and dealt in trash, or from those who offered fine articles at immoderate prices."[26] Lisner was a short, charismatic man who found a way to commercial success by offering quality, moderately priced goods on a cash-only basis. Within ten years, without adopting a credit structure for customers, Lisner's Palais Royal became one of Washington's largest stores.

When Lisner moved the business to the corner of Eleventh and G Streets in 1893, he was sharply criticized for not opening a location on F Street, Washington's main shopping street. He was confident that shoppers would follow him to G Street. The move was successful and Palais Royal "helped establish the [immediate] neighborhood as a viable [new] shopping district."[27] Lisner's store was one of the main reasons why Samuel Walter Woodward and Alvin Mason Lothrop moved their business to the Carlisle

The Palais Royal was Washington's first large department store when it opened its new location at Eleventh and G Streets NW in 1893. *Courtesy of the National Photo Company Collection at the Library of Congress.*

Building in 1877, across G Street from Palais Royal. The new shopping area also prospered because Washington's main streetcar line on G Street ran right between the two stores.

The Palais Royal store was considered "one of the most modern and complete of its kind south of New York City" when it opened on October 2, 1893. The four-story building contained twenty-foot-high ceilings, hardwood floors, large show windows and high Romanesque arches. "Palais Royal was the first big Washington store with some pretense, as compared to its competition," says historian Richard Longstreth. The store's popularity made Abram Lisner one of Washington's wealthiest citizens. He was the sole owner of Palais Royal and decided to retire from the business in 1924. He sold his department store to Kresge Department Stores of Newark, New Jersey. Kresge Department Stores was a separate company from the S.S. Kresge variety store chain, although the two retail divisions shared the direction of Sebastian S. Kresge. Mr. Kresge envisioned owning a large department store in every city that was home to a Kresge variety store. Kresge started his venture with the purchase of Newark's L.S. Plaut store and then purchased Washington's Palais Royal when he heard that Lisner was interested in selling. However, Kresge's dream of operating a nationwide holding group of major department stores never materialized.

Under Kresge's leadership, Palais Royal evolved into a moderately priced and promotional department store. From 1938 to 1942, Palais Royal was the home of the "mystifying and amazing" Kute Kris Kringle. Kute Kris Kringle was the brainchild of Broadway and Hollywood producer Mike Todd. Kringle was a three-inch-tall Santa Claus who was a "real" human, "not a midget, not a gnome, not a pigmy, not a Lilliputian." Todd created the illusion by using trick mirrors while children spoke to the "live" Kris Kringle on a telephone.[28] Palais Royal's Kute Kris Kringle exhibit was one of several that Todd leased to various department stores. In 1942, a 375-pound Santa Claus with a sixty-two-inch waistline joined Kringle. His "girth" was just as much a special Christmas attraction as the three-inch Kringle.

Palais Royal is credited as the first Washington department store to open a suburban branch operation. On September 30, 1942, a modest-sized Palais Royal opened at 7201 Wisconsin Avenue in Bethesda, Maryland. The store carried a limited offering of clothing, along with a selection of household goods. The branch was stocked with merchandise that was "hard to get in Bethesda, such as sheets, pillow cases, table linens and all

The Palais Royal's exclusive third-floor dress salon. *Courtesy of the National Photo Company Collection at the Library of Congress.*

types of bedding." The Bethesda branch was followed by a location at the Pentagon. The small Pentagon store opened on December 4, 1943. It was designed to serve the thirty thousand Pentagon workers who were working in "war-needed services" and needed a retail store close at hand. The store tended to rotate merchandise, and its employees were considered federal government employees, since it was located within the Pentagon building. "The Pentagon store was no bigger than my house," (says) former manager Shirley Mihursky. "It catered to lunch hour customers, and they knew their clientele. That's how they stocked that store." A small Palais Royal shop also operated at Arlington Farms, a temporary wartime housing complex for female civilian federal workers.

Reports circulated in early January 1946 that Woodward & Lothrop had made an offer to purchase Palais Royal for $5.7 million. The purchase price included the Palais Royal store, warehouse, merchandise and branches. Kresge shareholders approved the acquisition the following month, and Woodward & Lothrop took control of the Palais Royal operation on March 5. Most Palais Royal employees were offered employment at Woodward & Lothrop. However, upper management employees lost their jobs along with sixty black truck drivers and shipping clerks. Washingtonians had mixed feelings about the purchase of Palais Royal.

On the one hand, many felt it was a bad thing for an old and cherished institution like Palais Royal to be "swallowed up," obliterated in name and policy, so to speak. Other Washingtonians were glad that, since Palais Royal had been sold, Woodward & Lothrop had purchased it. Such feelings were difficult to resolve.[29]

"It was a valuable property and we didn't want to see somebody come in there and use it," says former Woodward & Lothrop president Waldo Burnside. "It wasn't part of a family and the management wasn't very aggressive. They didn't have the money to fully expand, and rather than meet the challenge, they decided to sell," said (says) Burnside. Reports surfaced that R.H. Macy Co. and Kobacker Stores of Ohio and New York expressed interest in Palais Royal. Alvin Lothrop's granddaughter, Nancy Orme, recalled (recalls) Palais Royal as "another sort of department store, but I don't think that it was as big or as well run as Woodward & Lothrop."

The Palais Royal purchase gave Woodward & Lothrop its first entry into running branch stores. It also provided new opportunities at the downtown location. The Palais Royal store was renamed the North Building. Woodward & Lothrop initially envisioned the North Building as a popular-priced apparel store, but it was eventually transitioned into a home furnishings and housewares

The Palais Royal Bethesda, Maryland branch became the Woodward & Lothrop Bethesda Budget Store after Woodies' acquired its competitor in 1946. *Courtesy of the Richard Longstreth Collection.*

Palais Royal's small location at the Pentagon was continued for many years as a Woodward & Lothrop branch. Because of its location, store workers were classified as federal employees. *Courtesy of the Richard Longstreth Collection.*

operation. Shopper Sally Rosen recalls the "plain" North Building as Woodward & Lothrop's "poor stepsister." Rosen adds that, "It wasn't anything fancy," but it was a destination for home goods, such as sheets, towels and pillowcases. Within a few years, construction of an underground tunnel that connected the Main and North Buildings under G Street began. The tunnel was eight and a half feet wide and seventy feet long. Completed in March 1952, the tunnel allowed shoppers to travel between buildings with "complete disregard for the outside elements, natural or man-made." The company called the tunnel "another pace-setting Woodward & Lothrop service."

Woodward & Lothrop was a family business, and members of the Woodward and Lothrop families had been involved in its management since the very beginning. In February 1942, at age fifty-three, store president Donald Woodward passed away after a long illness. William Wade Everett, a nephew of founder Samuel Walton Woodward, succeeded Donald Woodward. Everett served as the store president only until 1947, when his personal physicians insisted that he retire from the company's presidency due to high blood pressure. Everett's short tenure was noted for his successful acquisition of the Palais Royal store and its branches. He passed away in 1949 after suffering a cerebral hemorrhage.

Upon Everett's retirement, Andrew Parker, Walter Woodward's grandson, became the company president. Alvin Lothrop Luttrell, Alvin Mason Lothrop's grandson, joined Parker as the company's executive vice-president. Both men already had extensive experience working in the store, and both usually worked capably as a team. Upon assuming the presidency, Andy Parker said, "Teamwork is the one thing that is paramount to the success of an organization like ours."[30] Parker also credited the store's merchandising team with establishing "never-out" lists in various departments. One of Andy's sons, Brainard Parker, recalls visits to the downtown store with his father:

> *I remember walking around the store with my dad. What made it so special was that he knew every employee by name. He'd say, "Joe, how are you doing today?" The employees were delighted. My family was open and friendly with everybody. The other executives just acted like executives. But my father was very private. Once he left the store, he just wanted to spend time in the garden.*

Buyer Donald Godfrey says that Andy Parker was "wonderful, wonderful, wonderful." Godfrey continued: "Andy was a swell guy but he had some fetishes. He loved to make sure that all of the lights were on. If they didn't come on, he'd get pissed." Alvin Lothrop's great-grandson, Nathaniel Orme, says Andy was social and gregarious. However, Nathaniel's uncle, Alvin Lothrop Luttrell, nicknamed "Lotie," was "a nice fellow who was shy and reserved but very smart and studious." Donald Godfrey says, "[Lotie] was part of the day-to-day operations of the store. [Lotie] was more reserved and not as outgoing as Andy. If there was any dissention between the two of them, you'd never know it." The Woodward and Lothrop families never seemed stronger. In the book *From Founders to Grandsons*, the company praised the new leadership: "All of the years of accomplishment to bring a great store to its peak were climaxed when the grandsons of the Founders took the reins. Without doubt, it was more than Samuel Walter Woodward and Alvin Mason Lothrop could have hoped for."[31]

In 1949, Woodward & Lothrop began to make mention of itself as "Woodie's," with an apostrophe, in some of its advertisements. Washingtonians had been affectionately calling the store "Woodies" for years. Former president Waldo Burnside says, "We called ourselves Woodies, and we didn't have the feeling that tradition says otherwise. We would go to manufacturers, and we would hear them say 'Woodburn & Lathrop.' It was a tongue twister." In November 1950, the company debuted its new children's television show, *Playtime*, on WNBW-TV. The half-hour show featured "the thrilling adventures of 'Woodie' and 'Lotie' who 'live' right here at Woodies." The store also produced *Something New* on WTOP-TV and *Across the Counter*, featuring shopping hints for the whole family, on WMAL-TV. In 1984, a woman from Chevy Chase wrote an editorial in the *Washington Post* with the headline "Old-Timers Don't Say Woodies." She argued:

> *When I was a small child (before World War I), a few of my mother's elderly friends still called it "the Boston Store"...Everyone else called it Woodward & Lothrop's. "Woodies?" Good heavens, No! Nobody would have dreamed of applying a chummy familiar nickname to that staid and sober establishment...It was not until the 1960s that I first heard it referred to as "Woodies," and then by teen-agers who were too lazy to utter five syllables. And it was a long time after that before the store itself succumbed and began using "Woodies" in its ads. As for me, I still say Woodward & Lothrop's.*[32]

But the reader was wrong. Woodward & Lothrop's family members, executives, employees and shoppers found the Woodies nickname to be endearing. Nancy Orme had no problem with the name Woodies, although it didn't acknowledge the Lothrop name: "The name Woodies was all right with me."

Washington Shopping Plate

W oodies was like Peoples Drug, people just loved it," says historian
John DeFerrari. Woodies wasn't the only department store that
anchored Washington's F Street shopping corridor. Large retailers such as
Garfinckel's, the Hecht Company, Lansburgh's, Kann's and Jelleff's made F
Street a regional shopping destination. "Woodies had a location advantage,"
says Waldo Burnside. "Hecht's was farthest from the center of shopping, and
they were at a disadvantage." Woodies' show windows also played a huge
role in the success of the store. "We sold a lot of merchandise from those
windows," says Burnside. However, up until 1947, Woodward & Lothrop
covered its show windows on Sundays with large black drapes. The company
felt that it was morally necessary to hide its wares on Sundays. "We didn't
even advertise in the *Washington Post* on Sundays because of their liquor
advertising," says Burnside. That policy eventually changed, and Woodward
& Lothrop enjoyed a premiere status with the *Post*. Former company president
Robert B. Mang says that one of his most enjoyable times at Woodies was
the relationship the store had with the paper:

> *We had a fantastic relationship with the* Washington Post. *Once when
> the* Post *was struggling, the paper came to Woodies and said, "If you'll
> advertise every day of the year, we'll give you a prominent location in the
> paper." We always had page three. Hecht's complained about Woodies
> guarantee of a spot on page three. They were very jealous because they did
> more advertising in the* Post.

Woodward & Lothrop's centralized location also made the store a popular meeting place for shoppers. "When you came into the store off G Street, across from Palais Royal, there was a balcony," said Burnside. "There were women who loved to sit up there. Some women complained when somebody was sitting in 'their' seat." Woodies' centralized location on F Street also mirrored its image as a department store with moderate to better merchandise. By the 1940s, Woodies' competitors decided to expand into Washington's suburbs as the city grew in size. Suburban growth helped retailers expand their sales, but it was also at the expense of their large downtown flagships. "Department stores started as one-stop shopping centers that carried everything from toothpaste to furniture," says Burnside. "But that all changed when the stores opened suburban branch stores." Shoppers seemed willing to exchange vast assortments of merchandise selection for longer hours and free parking. Garfinckel's was the first large store to open a suburban location, but the Hecht Company perfected suburban expansion with its large, complete and stylish branch stores. Nonetheless, all of Washington's major stores had their own clientele and their own place in the market. "Garfinckel's was more staid and was seen as 'the mother of the bride.' Woodies was the bride, and Hecht's was the bridesmaid," says Woodies' former media spokesperson Robbie Snow.

In October 1950, an organization called the Washington Shopping Plate Associates was formed. This new cooperative combined the individual charge accounts of six large Washington retailers into one identification plate with a single account number. The Hecht Company, Jelleff's, Kann's, Lansburgh's, Raleigh Haberdasher and Woodward & Lothrop were partners in this new credit program. Garfinckel's joined the shopping plate system at a later date. Within a few months, every Washington store charge customer was mailed the new Washington Shopping Plate. The tiny one-and-a-half by two-and-a-half-inch metal plate was accompanied by its own "simulated" leather case. The Washington Shopping Plate gave customers "assurance of accuracy in handling transactions…a guarantee of welcome…and best of all, the greatest time saver and annoyance saver." It was a promise of "modern streamlined shopping." Participating stores accepted the Washington Shopping Plate well into the mid-1990s, even though the associates disbanded the Shopping Plate a decade earlier. Hecht's and Woodward & Lothrop kept Shopping Plate customer account numbers active. Hecht's executive office said in 1995, "There are some people who just like to use their Shopping Plate, so we'll take it, no problem. People who have been customers for 40 or 50 years just like things the same way they've always been." It was just another sign of deep loyalty that shoppers had for "their" stores.

JULIUS GARFINCKEL & CO.

"There was something so glamorous about Garfinckel's," says Washingtonian and fashion icon Tim Gunn. "I liked Garfinckel's because it had dim lighting, and it seemed a little more intimate than the other stores. It was the go-to place for family Christmas gifts. Customers who frequented the upper-end large retail stores throughout Europe felt at home at Garfinckel's. Garfinckel's was not a standard department store; it was a large quality [and] specialty [store] that carried some of Washington's finest ready-to-wear clothing, in an addition to a distinctive home and gift department. It was 'the Pearl' of F Street, where shopping had a touch of class."

Julius Garfinkle & Co., "featuring imported novelties and specialties," opened for business on October 2, 1905, at 1226 F Street. As the former manager of the ladies' department at Parker, Bridget & Co., Julius Garfinkle

An exterior view of Garfinckel's stately downtown store at the corner of Fourteenth and F Streets from 1966. *Courtesy of the D.C. Public Library, Washingtoniana Division.*

was well known to female Washingtonians seeking the latest in fashion. He was a hardworking merchant whom other merchants "came to regard… as having remarkable ability in picking women's clothes and many of his customers consulted him personally about their selections."[33] By 1912, Garfinkle slowly incorporated his given name, spelled "Garfinckel," into his store's advertisements. Successful from the start, Julius Garfinckel had a "scrupulous regard for business ethics and a justifiable pride." He managed his high-end store without displaying any signage indicating special sales. This was a tradition that lasted throughout much of its existence. On October 6, 1930, Julius Garfinckel moved his thriving business into an elegant nine-story building at the corner of Fourteenth and F Streets. Garfinckel added men's and boys' clothing, luggage, jewelry and silverware at its new location, in addition to women's wear and "allied lines." At the store's opening, the *Washington Post* reported, "When the doors are opened to the public, it is safe to predict that one of the most beautiful stores in Washington will be on view." The paper continued, "Beauty of proportions, grace of line and dignity of balance are all combined in this new mercantile establishment."[34]

On August 17, 1942, Julius Garfinckel & Co. opened its Spring Valley store at the intersection of Massachusetts Avenue and Fordham Road. The company was the first major downtown Washington store to open a suburban location. Garfinckel did not intend to operate it as a branch store. The company referred to it as a replica of the downtown store, complete in every way except on a smaller scale. The opening day advertisement praised the company's achievement.

> *All the charm of old Williamsburg set down at the edge of a dark, cool forest…but our modern job of good store-keeping shows up in modern details—a large parking lot, complete air-conditioning, an outside blackout switch. It's way above the average as suburban stores go.*[35]

Garfinckel at Spring Valley included a branch of the downtown Antoine Salon, the company's signature beauty salon. In 1951, Garfinckel considered an expansion to Wilmington, Delaware's Merchandise Mart, based on its suburban success in Spring Valley. Unfortunately, the plan never materialized. Garfinckel continued its suburban expansion at Seven Corners in Falls Church, Virginia (1956); Montgomery Mall (1968); Tysons Corner (1969); Landover Mall (1972); Springfield Mall (1973); and the Annapolis Mall (1980).

Garfinckel's store in Spring Valley, Maryland, became the first downtown Washington store to expand into the suburbs. *Courtesy of the Richard Longstreth Collection*.

In addition to its spread throughout suburban Washington, Julius Garfinckel & Co. acquired a number of prominent retailers. Garfinckel purchased Brooks Brothers in May 1946. Brooks Brothers was founded in 1818 and is still today considered one of the nation's oldest retail stores. At the time of its purchase, Brooks Brothers consisted of one store, located on New York's Madison Avenue shopping district. It was not until 1968 that Brooks Brothers had a Washington presence. In 1950, Garfinckel purchased A. De Pinna Co., a fashionable clothing retailer that dated from 1885. The De Pinna purchase included a main store on New York's Fifth Avenue; New Haven, Connecticut; and seasonal shops in Magnolia, Massachusetts, and Miami Beach, Florida. On April 27, 1967, Garfinckel's announced a merger agreement with Miller & Rhoads of Richmond, Virginia. Miller & Rhoads was a beloved retail institution that consisted of large downtown stores in Richmond, Roanoke and Charlottesville, in addition to several other Virginia cities. Other acquisitions included Miller's of Knoxville (1968), Miller Brothers of Chattanooga, the high-fashion contemporary clothing chain Ann Taylor (1977) and Kansas City's Harzfeld's specialty store chain (1972). In addition to all the aforementioned purchases, Garfinckel acquired Washington's Joseph R. Harris Co. stores in 1971. Founded in 1916,

Joseph R. Harris sold "moderately priced merchandise in a higher-priced atmosphere."[36] It operated eleven women's clothing stores in Washington, Charlotte and Atlanta. The marriage between the Garfinckel and Joseph R. Harris stores was less than ideal. Garfinckel tried to position the Harris stores toward a younger and more budget-minded audience, and Harris officials became entangled in a possible takeover dispute with Garfinckel's top management. The stores, renamed Harris & Friends, were sold to Petrie Stores in 1979.

Woodies' management and customers tended to align Woodward & Lothrop with Garfinckel's rather than any other Washington store. Former Woodies buyer Allison Godfrey feels "the only store above us was Garfinckel's, but they had a little snob appeal." Nancy Orme says, "I think that [Woodward & Lothrop's] only competition was Garfinckel's." Former Woodward & Lothrop president Edwin Hoffman admired Garfinckel's role in the city's retail culture: "Woodward & Lothrop respected Garfinckel's, and we pecked away at what they did well." He acknowledges that running an upscale retailer such as Garfinckel's can pose challenges to a company's bottom line. "When you get into high-end merchandise, you limit your customers," states Hoffman. Woodward & Lothrop offered all types of goods to all types of customers. Although its designer offerings competed with Garfinckel's, Woodward & Lothrop found its niche by trading to a broader customer base. "Garfinckel's was like Neiman-Marcus, Woodward & Lothrop was like Bloomingdale's and Hecht's was like Macy's," says fashion expert Tim Gunn.

THE HECHT COMPANY

Samuel Hecht and his family had been a major part of Baltimore's business scene for almost forty years before they decided to try their luck in Washington. In 1857, Samuel Hecht established his first retail store in Baltimore's Fell's Point neighborhood. The store and the family continued its Baltimore growth for many years, and by 1861, more than eight Hecht family-run businesses operated in East Baltimore. Samuel's son Moses Hecht became the family's driving business force and established a full-line department store called Hecht Brothers in Baltimore's downtown. Located at the intersection of Baltimore and Pine Streets, Hecht Brothers opened in 1885 and established a loyal clientele who traded mostly through credit, "the

Poor Man's Friend." On March 21, 1896, Moses Hecht, and his brother Alexander, opened Hecht & Company at 515 Seventh Street in downtown Washington. Hecht & Company's business was based on credit, and the company advertised, "Hundreds and hundreds of Baltimore home-holders are enjoying this accommodation—hundreds of Washington home-holders will share it when they know more about its benefits—its liberality." Like Woodward & Lothrop, Hecht & Company offered a satisfaction guarantee along with a one-price system, but unlike Woodward & Lothrop, Hecht publicized that it would "never ask [the customer] to pay cash for anything" and that its policies made the company the "most liberal merchant in the country."[37] Hecht's targeted market was white- and blue-collar customers of moderate income. Its success was based on well-known merchandise complemented by an aggressive merchandising campaign. The company's sales steadily grew, and by World War II, Hecht closely trailed Woodward & Lothrop in sales volume.[38]

Although stores such as Garfinckel's and Woodward & Lothrop offered higher-end merchandise than the Hecht Company, the store claimed in 1956 that "the families which have occupied the [White House] since President Franklin D. Roosevelt have been on its customer list." One of its earliest customers was Mrs. Calvin Coolidge, who selected a pair of shoes and asked if she could charge her purchase.

"Do you have a charge account here?" the clerk asked Mrs. Coolidge. Mrs. Coolidge said she did not. The clerk guided her to the credit department, where the customer's address, 1600 Pennsylvania Avenue, touched a responsive chord in the credit clerk's memory. "You mean the White House?" the clerk gasped.[39]

The store recovered from the embarrassment. As its business continued its growth, the Hecht Company expanded into a new large ornate building at Seventh and F Streets NW in 1925 and promoted its new brand-name merchandise. Over the years, Hecht's established the city's first complete escalator service (1936) and was the first store to open a parking garage (1937). But most importantly, the Hecht Company became the first retailer to open a complete suburban department store branch in the Washington suburbs.

Woodies' former president Waldo Burnside recalls, "When branch stores came to be, Hecht's was the first, and it gave them a giant step." The Hecht Company opened a $2.5 million store in Silver Spring, Maryland, on November 1, 1947. At the time, Silver Spring was credited as being one of the fastest-growing areas not only in greater Washington but also on the East Coast.[40] Two thousand customers showed up to the store's opening festivities, and

GALA OPENING SATURDAY, NOVEMBER 1st.
10 A.M. to 9 P.M.

THE HECHT CO.
SILVER SPRING

A complete department store serving Northwest Washington and Maryland.
116 departments featuring fine merchandise bearing nationally famous labels.
Ultra modern, bright, colorful . . . streamlined for new shopping pleasure.

Left: The downtown Hecht Company store operated out of its classic Seventh Street building until 1985. *Courtesy of the Richard Longstreth Collection.*

Right: The Hecht Company store in Silver Spring, Maryland, became the area's first full-line suburban department store when it opened on November 1, 1947. *Courtesy of the Richard Longstreth Collection.*

Maryland governor William Preston Lane Jr. said the new Hecht Company Silver Spring store was a sign of "faith in the future of Maryland." Upon its opening, the Silver Spring Hecht's was the largest department store on the eastern seaboard outside a downtown city shopping core.[41]

The company followed up its Silver Spring suburban success with a store in Arlington County, Virginia. On November 2, 1951, sixty thousand customers came to the grand opening of Hecht's PARKington store at Glebe Road and Wilson Boulevard. It boasted being "the largest suburban department store in the East" and was attached to "the nation's largest parking building."[42] The garage provided free two-hour parking for Hecht shoppers and offered a new arrangement that allowed customers to enter the store on the level that they parked. The store featured an illuminated façade that displayed store promotions, much to the dismay of nearby residents. The company appeased its concerned neighbors by only displaying messages on community service organizations instead of merchandising events.[43] Hecht's suburban expansion continued with its new Prince George's Plaza store in November 1958. The Plaza store followed a more conventional design than its predecessors, and the company redirected its focus on moderate-income customers and basic, reliable, name-brand merchandise.[44] Hecht's had previously announced that its fourth Washington-area location would be located on Wisconsin Avenue in the Somerset neighborhood, but the company abandoned its plans after vigorous neighborhood protests. The Prince George's Plaza store and adjacent shopping center was built on the site of the former Christian Heurich estate. Heurich's company was the brewer and distributor of the popular Senate Beer and Old Georgetown Ale brands.

The Hecht Company's successful suburban branch stores in Washington and Baltimore caught the attention of the May Company department store group. May saw the success and future of department stores in America's suburbs and not in downtown areas. In October 1958, May and Hecht merged their organizations and created a regional powerhouse. May continued Hecht's Washington growth with stores in Marlow Heights (August 1960),

Hecht's PARKington store on Glebe Road in Arlington, Virginia, became a driving suburban shopping source in 1951. The store claimed to be attached to the nation's largest parking garage. The revamped shopping center later assumed the name Ballston Common. *Courtesy of the Richard Longstreth Collection.*

the Laurel Shopping Center (April 1964), Alexandria's Landmark Shopping Center (August 1965), Tysons Corner (July 1968), Montgomery Mall (March 1968) and Landover Mall (May 1972). During its time of expansion in the Washington suburbs, the Hecht Company slowly changed, specifically with assistance and support from its May Company parent. Woodies former executive vice-president Howard Lehrer says, "Hecht's upgraded very selectively and with thought behind it. Woodies just stood still." By the early 1970s, the Hecht Company was Woodies' greatest competitor. Although, Woodies former president Robert B. Mang says, "Hecht's didn't have the brands [that Woodies' had]." Longtime Woodies' president Edwin Hoffman feels that Woodward & Lothrop lost a lot of market share to the Hecht Company. Hoffman stated, "Hecht's was our biggest threat," and by the mid-1970s, "there wasn't a tremendous amount of difference between Woodward & Lothrop and Hecht's."

Lansburgh's

Similar to the Hecht Company, Lansburgh's origins stem from a successful stint in the neighboring city of Baltimore. Gustave Lansburgh and his brother James opened his Baltimore dry goods store in 1854. Lansburgh brothers expanded to Washington in 1860 and opened a small business on the second floor of the Bank of Washington at Seventh Street and Louisiana Avenue. These humble beginnings paved the way for one of the largest department stores in Washington. In 1863, Lansburgh moved into a street-level storefront near Seventh and D Streets. Accompanied by his brother Max, the new name of the business became "Lansburgh & Bro's Baltimore Bargain Store." Even from a very early start, Lansburgh's stressed modestly priced merchandise, which led to its success, especially during the nation's economic struggles.

One of the company's greatest contributions was the role that it played after the assassination of President Abraham Lincoln in 1865. Washington immediately went into mourning following his death, but the city did not have an ample supply of black fabric and goods for appropriate clothing wear. Lansburgh immediately traveled to Baltimore, purchased every piece of black fabric that he could and sold it to government workers and private citizens. The *Washington Post* called Lansburgh's action "a merchandising 'beat' little short of brilliance: the entire city had to go to Lansburgh's."[45]

The store gradually expanded along Seventh Street until it opened its final completed structure on March 10, 1925. Over 850 workers were employed in the 220,000-square-foot store.

In July 1951, the City Stores Corporation purchased Lansburgh's, and the store passed out of the family's hands. City Stores also owned other retailers such as Philadelphia's Lit Brothers, New Orleans's Maison Blanche and Memphis's Richards department stores. Lansburgh's remained quiet under City Stores's control. The company believed its downtown store would "retain its own" and that "suburban stores merely provide for a new growth."[46] Lansburgh's was the last large Washington department to open a suburban store. Its Langley Park store opened on October 17, 1955, at the intersection of New Hampshire Avenue and University Lane and earned the title of Prince George's County's first department store. The Langley Park branch was followed by a location at the Shirlington Shopping Center on September 14, 1959. One of the company's greatest challenges was its fight to become an original anchor store at the new Tysons Corner Shopping Center. Lansburgh's claimed that it was promised an anchor location at Tysons Corner but that mall management changed its mind after the shopping center won zoning approval. The fight played out in the courts for a number of years, and Lansburgh's finally joined Tysons Corner one year after the center's grand opening. The large Tysons Corner location did not meet its sales expectations, and the company blamed its late arrival into the center as the main source of its troubles.

Lansburgh's targeted its store for the "middle-of-the-road" customer, but by the late 1960s, the company was not only fighting the Hecht Company and Woodward & Lothrop for market share but was also struggling against competition from discounters such as Zayre, K-Mart and Memco. A former Woodies executive recalled, "We didn't even know that Lansburgh's was there." Lansburgh's believed "merchandise doesn't have to be expensive to be in good taste," but that seemed to be a losing policy.[47] One retail analyst stated, "Lansburgh's basement trade was excellent, or at least good, but the upper floors, designed to serve the middle class, were deserted."[48] Lansburgh's stopped pulling a profit in 1967, but it still opened two more suburban locations. A store in downtown Rockville, Maryland, part of a new business core called Rockville Town Center, opened in February 1972 and immediately faced stiff competition from nearby Montgomery Mall and Wheaton Plaza. Another Lansburgh's opened in February 1973 at the Springfield

This image shows the Eighth and E Streets corner of the downtown Lansburgh's department store. Lansburgh's catered to Washington's moderate customer until its closure in 1973. *Courtesy of the Richard Longstreth Collection.*

Mall. By the time the Springfield store opened, it was no secret that Lansburgh's was in financial trouble. Its president George Joint stated at the Springfield opening, "We have no intention of fighting Garfinckel's, or Woodies, or Hecht's for business in higher-priced merchandise. We can offer the right fashions and style for a lot less."[49] Two months later, the fight was over. Lansburgh's, the store that didn't take chances and failed to change with the times, began its final closure in May 1973.

KANN'S

"Kann's was probably on par with Lansburgh's, but Lansburgh's was maybe a slight step above," said Donald Godrey, a former buyer for Woodward & Lothrop. "Kann's was known for its home merchandise and had a good domestics department. Lansburgh's was more about apparel than home goods." Like Lansburgh's, Kann's came to Washington after many successful years of operation in neighboring Baltimore. Solomon Kann established his Baltimore store in 1862 in the city's Fell's Point neighborhood. Kann's became known as the "cheapest store in Baltimore," and it offered "tremendous values that no sensible lady would be slow to jump at." The Baltimore store originally operated as "Sol'n J. Kann & Co.," but Solomon soon brought his sons—Louis, Sigmund and Simon—into the business. In 1893, Kann's sons traveled to Washington and purchased the unsold merchandise of the bankrupt A. Kaufman store. On July 5, Washington's S. Kann, Sons Co. opened for business.

Kann's was known as "the Busy Corner" and established its prominence at Eighth Street and Pennsylvania Avenue. By the 1950s, S. Kann, Sons Co. contained over 200,000 square feet of selling space spread throughout fifteen connected buildings. On November 16, 1951, Kann's opened its first and only suburban store with a 120,000-square-foot location at North Fairfax Drive and North Kirkwood Street in Arlington, Virginia. The company advertised, "For many of you fortunates who live in nearby residential sections of Clarendon, a little walk for Junior can combine with a little shopping treat at Kann's for you."[50] Kann's remained committed to its downtown Washington store and installed sheets of gray aluminum siding on its storefront in 1959, much to the concern of the city's fine arts commission. The store felt that it was necessary to update and modernize the exterior of its business in order to give a modern and competitive image to downtown shoppers.

The company remained stagnant throughout the 1960s and acknowledged that its "expansion in the suburban areas has not been as pronounced as some of our older and newer department and department-like stores."[51] After falling to a very distant fourth in sales among Washington's complete department stores, Kann's was purchased by the L.S. Good & Co. department store group in December 1971. Based in Wheeling, West Virginia, Good operated several middle-range department stores in smaller cities such as Smith-Bridgman's of Flint, Michigan, and Gable's of Altoona, Pennsylvania. Despite investing over $800,000 in renovations within its two Washington-area stores, Kann's announced its final closure on May 21, 1975. Experts blamed its lack of suburban expansion, lack of aggressive management and antiquated downtown structure for its financial troubles. At the time of Kann's closure, Woodies president Edwin Hoffman said, "[Kann's closure] was very unhealthy for the economic vitality of downtown. I thought Kann's had a pretty good piece of the market. I'm surprised and distressed."[52] The final nail in the coffin occurred on March 31, 1979, when the vacant downtown Kann's store fell victim to Washington's largest fire in over thirty years. The aluminum panels that were installed on the building's exterior

Kann's, an important Eighth Street department store, opened its only suburban location at Arlington, Virginia, in 1951. It was quickly overshadowed by Hecht Company's PARKington store. *Courtesy of the Richard Longstreth Collection.*

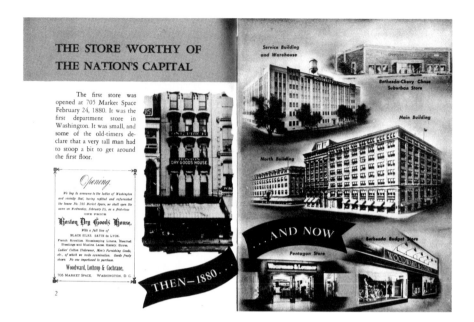

This 1950 advertisement shows all Woodward & Lothrop properties, including the Service Building, Bethesda locations and newly acquired Palais Royal stores. *Collection of the author.*

in 1959, intended to give the store its new modern appearance, prevented firefighters from effectively battling the blaze. The blaze "spread from the basement to the top floor in 10 seconds," and the fire was extinguished through the help of power saws and air chisels that removed the building's aluminum exterior.

March to the Beltway

After the end of World War II, America entered a period of growth and prosperity. America's downtown shopping areas produced strong sales, but many customers began to look beyond the city limits for housing.

Many downtown retailers decided to follow their customers and build locations in the suburbs. The first round of American branch department stores that were built immediately following the war were popular and profitable. These stores did not tend to undercut sales at their downtown flagships.[53] However, many department stores were fearful that suburban expansion could undermine their significant investments in their downtown flagships. But these same large local stores were also afraid that national retailers, such as Sears, Roebuck, would locate stores outside the city limits and undercut their hard-won market shares.[54]

By 1948, Washington was already suffering from traffic congestion on many of the city's roadways. Downtown retailers pressed the need for street straightening and widening in order to maintain retail trade with visiting suburban residents. The area's Capital Beltway was still about a decade away from construction, and Washington's downtown department stores initially set their sights on the northern Maryland suburbs for retail expansion. The population growth and economic stability of communities such as Silver Spring, Bethesda and Arlington justified the need for suburban department stores that offered comprehensive assortments of merchandise.[55]

In August 1945, Woodward & Lothrop quietly announced plans for its first suburban store, located at Wisconsin and Western Avenues in Chevy

A postcard image of Woodward & Lothrop's fine gift shop on the downtown store's fifth floor. *Collection of the author.*

The store's exclusive Silver Room was a destination for many Washingtonian shoppers. *Collection of the author.*

Chase, Maryland, just past the District border. Chevy Chase was one of Washington's many prosperous suburbs, and the area lacked suitable shopping options. With the store's announcement, Woodward & Lothrop stated, "Rich in historical tradition, Montgomery County comes naturally by its wonderful people and progressive institutions."[56] Work started on the location in October 1949, and the store celebrated its grand opening on November 2, 1950. Members of the Woodward and Lothrop families joined local dignitaries and politicians at the celebration. Mrs. Margaret Welsh cut the maroon satin ribbon on opening day. Walsh, age ninety-four at the ceremony, was Woodward & Lothrop's very first customer at its location at 921 Pennsylvania on January 1, 1881. The new $2 million store contained over 100,000 square feet on three levels. The modern Georgian-designed store "combined contemporary, future and classical beauty" and offered free parking for five hundred automobiles. A cornerstone containing a capsule of earth from the groundbreaking, a Woodlothian magazine, a tube of corn kernels (symbolic of growth) and newspaper clippings were contained in the stone.[57]

The Chevy Chase store was about "location, location, location," says former president Waldo Burnside. "It was our first branch store, and it was sensational. It was strategically located and had a good customer makeup." The location ended up appealing to the affluent local customer base. "For people in Chevy Chase, Northern Virginia and Potomac, it was their store," recalls former vice-chairman Robert Mulligan. Buyer Donald Godfrey says, "Chevy Chase was fabulous. You would get customers who had homes in the Bahamas come in and spend $2,000 in candles just so they made sure that they'd have candlelight at dinnertime in the Bahamas! It was a great store." Woodies soon outgrew its Chevy Chase location. "The one problem with the Chevy Chase store was that it became too small," says Burnside. "We tried to make a deal to get more parking, but we weren't able to work that out." In 1966, Woodies enlarged its Chevy Chase location with a two-story, 100,000-square-foot addition.

Founder Walter Woodward's great-grandson Brainard Parker kept a very low profile as a member of the Woodward family. Although he resided near the Chevy Chase store, very few of Brainard's friends knew of his relationship to the store, and those who did assumed that he could get anything for friends. He remembers one visit to the Chevy Chase location with some of his friends:

An early image of Woodward & Lothrop's popular Bethesda–Chevy Chase store along Wisconsin Avenue. *Courtesy of the Richard Longstreth Collection.*

A classic view of Chevy Chase store's side portico. *Courtesy of the Richard Longstreth Collection.*

I stopped by the Chevy Chase store one day after school with two other guys. One of the guys showed me a charm bracelet that he just took off of the counter. I thought, "Holy shit, I got to get out of here!" I wasn't going to tell him who my family was. I didn't want to go there, so I just hustled him out of the store.

Neither Brainard Parker nor his brother Andrew Parker Jr. ever went to work in the family business.

Woodward & Lothrop selected Arlington, Virginia, as the site of its next suburban store. Woodies planned a four-story, 150,000-square-foot store in the 400 block of Glebe Road. The land purchase was contingent on a rezoning from residential to commercial construction. Several local Arlington residents vehemently opposed the Arlington store. Residents filed suit, saying that the large store would create traffic congestion, endanger children, invade privacy rights and greatly reduce property values.

For almost six years, the Arlington store's fate was played in and out of the local court system. In September 1952, Woodies finally abandoned its plans in Arlington but followed through on a smaller store in Alexandria. On November 28, 1952, Woodward & Lothrop opened a thirty-one-

A rare sketching of Woodies' proposed Arlington, Virginia location. Neighbors protested the store's construction and the project was abandoned in September 1952. *Courtesy of the Richard Longstreth Collection.*

Woodward & Lothrop's first sizable Virginia location was located in downtown Alexandria. It opened for business in November 1952 and was later overshadowed by the Landmark Center store. *Courtesy of the Richard Longstreth Collection.*

thousand-square-foot, three-story store at 615 Washington Street in Alexandria. The store was much smaller in size than the proposed Arlington location. The new store offered a "streamlined" selection of merchandise and "service with a worthy-of-Virginia tradition."[58] Mrs. George Warfield cut the ribbon for the new store. Warfield, a customer since 1888, was the Alexandrian with the oldest Woodward & Lothrop charge account, having opened it in 1910.

When Woodward & Lothrop purchased Palais Royal in 1946, it inherited the rights and leases to Palais Royal's three branch locations at the Pentagon, Arlington Farms and Bethesda. The small Arlington Farms shop was closed in mid-1948, but the Bethesda store was converted into a Budget Store. The Bethesda store was located about two miles north of Woodies' new Chevy Chase location, and Bethesda's conversion into a budget store made the two stores noncompetitive. However, on December 15, 1954, a massive fire destroyed the Bethesda Budget Store. The blaze caused $500,000 in damage and displaced its forty-five employees. The *Washington Star* newspaper reported, "Remnants of the Christmas displays were scattered along the sidewalk…Rudolph was found with his nose burned off and leaning against a parking meter. Parking meters were seared black and electrical wires were melted."[59] Firefighters fought to save the Woolworth store located next door. Woodward & Lothrop was committed to rebuilding the store because "it liked Bethesda and the Bethesda people." A new larger Bethesda Budget Store opened on September 6, 1955. The new building was air-conditioned, fireproof and expanded by one floor.

After a disastrous fire in December 1954, Woodward & Lothrop rebuilt its Bethesda Budget Store and added a second floor. *Courtesy of the Richard Longstreth Collection.*

Woodward & Lothrop began 1955 with a diamond jubilee celebration. Hundreds of merchants and manufacturers sent accolades that recognized the occasion to the company. On January 2, 1955, Woodward & Lothrop acknowledged its seventy-fifth anniversary in a full-paged newspaper advertisement:

> *Over the years, we have made many friends who have given us the affectionate nickname, "Woodies." Perhaps it is because Washington knows that the Woodward and Lothrop families maintain the founders' policies of fine merchandise and fair practices. Now we begin our year-long celebration with special emphasis on the beautiful fashions, handsome menswear, youngsters' clothing and outstanding home furnishings our leading resources constantly supply for you. Thanks to them, to the whole "Woodies' family" and to you…we're a great store…worthy of the Nation's Capital.*

The company's diamond jubilee included many special events held throughout the year. The Easter season featured "Bunnyville," which included visits by Bertram Bunny, along with egg-coloring contests and live animals. Other events included a Camellia Group, featuring exhibits by thirteen local Potomac Valley gardening groups, a Lily Fashionata show that benefitted an Easter Seals drive and "festivals of song" held on the store's G Street balcony during the Easter and Christmas seasons. Woodies received printed praise from department stores that were members of Frederick Atkins, Inc. Woodward & Lothrop joined the Frederick Atkins buying group in 1951 in order to obtain volume discount purchases and to gain access to industry-wide marketing research. A number of the country's largest department stores, such as John Wanamaker in Philadelphia and G. Fox & Co. in Hartford, enjoyed the buying resources of Frederick Atkins, Inc.

Sales and profits at Woodward & Lothrop continued to grow during this time. Annual sales approached $50 million in 1955, a gain of 5.5 percent from the previous year.[60] At the same time, many American department stores, including Woodward & Lothrop, revolutionized the way they practiced business. "We were trying to make the store more user friendly," says Waldo Burnside. In order to increase productivity in the downtown and suburban locations, department stores became more convenience oriented and less service oriented. "We went from showing everything in a case where customers couldn't reach the merchandise to turning around the cases and putting out the racks." The practice lowered expenses, but it disappointed many loyal customers. "When the customers lost service, it was worse than if they didn't ever have it to begin with," says Burnside. Alvin Lothrop's great-grandson Nathaniel Orme adds, "I don't think that department stores adapted as well as they could have. Woodward & Lothrop was a very good leader in Washington's department store business in the early 1950s and 1960s because they didn't have the competition." By the 1960s, many department stores showed sales declines as discounters entered the field. Discount stores offered many advantages, including low prices and customer convenience, and a number of traditional retailers were "priced out." But throughout the 1950s and 1960s, Washingtonians remained loyal to Woodies. The company posted increased sales and profits. In 1959, sales at all downtown Washington department stores had decreased from 5 to 15 percent over the past decade, except for at Woodies, whose downtown store increased its sales volume by 5 percent.

Woodward & Lothrop opened its second Virginia location on September 20, 1956, with a large store at the $15 million Seven Corners Shopping Center in Falls Church. At the time of the opening, Seven Corners was "the

Andrew Parker (left) and Alvin Lothrop Luttrell (right) pose for a photograph for the company's 1957 Annual Report. *Courtesy of the Historical Society of Washington, D.C.*

A Christmastime view of the information booth on the store's main floor during the mid-1950s. *Courtesy of the Historical Society of Washington, D.C.*

largest regional shopping center in Virginia and one of the largest on the Eastern Seaboard." Seven Corners management boasted that it was "the first shopping center in the United States in which one large department store is not dominant."[61] The center's "I-shaped design" was designed to "keep with the traditions of the home county of George Washington." An eight-story illuminated sign featured a large number "7" that changed colors as the weather changed. A bar of light flashed upward when the temperature increased and downward when the temperature dropped. The sign, along with its large digital clock, became a Northern Virginia landmark. Woodies and Julius Garfinckel & Co. were the two anchor stores at Seven Corners. Woodies' Seven Corners location "used color, line and fixtures with special 'woman appeal' and even installed pink telephones throughout the store." For decades, the Seven Corners store was a very profitable location for the company, but its clientele was quite different from that of the Chevy Chase store. Former media spokesperson Robbie Snow explains that "the Chevy Chase area was home to a lot of diplomats and heads of agencies. The area around Seven Corners was different because it was home to their secretaries. It was a true middle-class store."

Woodies continued its search for new suburban locations, and the department store took a second look in the northern Maryland suburbs. The company felt that the Wheaton-Kensington area showed phenomenal population growth and ideal potential.[62] The location was served by an improved and widened local road system and had close access to the new Capital Beltway. Woodward & Lothrop's Wheaton Plaza store opened on February 5, 1960. The 160,000-square-foot location joined the country's largest Montgomery Ward, along with a Giant Food, Hot Shoppes, seventy-five smaller stores and parking for five thousand automobiles. At more than one million square feet of retail space, Wheaton Plaza was the largest shopping center in the Washington metropolitan area.

Brainard Parker remembers attending the grand opening at Wheaton Plaza, in addition to the openings in Chevy Chase, Alexandria and Seven Corners. "The company passed out commemorative sterling silver Kirk

Delivery trucks announce, "We're on our way to Virginia!" for the opening of Woodward & Lothrop's Seven Corners store in September 1956. *Courtesy of the D.C. Public Library, Washingtoniana Division.*

Seven Corners, located in Falls Church, Virginia, proclaimed that it was the country's first suburban shopping center with two large anchor stores. Its signature sign was a beacon for Northern Virginia shoppers and residents. This image shows the Julius Garfinckel store in the foreground and the Woodies store at the far end. *Courtesy of the Richard Longstreth Collection.*

letter openings to the first customers in Wheaton. Imagine doing something like that today?" says Parker. Woodward & Lothrop was careful to tailor each store to its local demographic. Although the Wheaton store was only about six miles from the Chevy Chase store, separate buyers were employed at each location. Chevy Chase offered decidedly more upscale merchandise than Wheaton but "there was a small group that shopped both Chevy Chase and Wheaton," says Waldo Burnside.

The company made an unusual move in October 1963 when it opened a junior department store at the Eastover Shopping Center in Prince George's County. Originally marketed specifically as a Budget Store, the 47,250-square-foot Eastover store opened as an official Woodward & Lothrop branch but concentrated on "fresh dollar-stretching merchandise for easy self selection." Unlike the other suburban stores, Eastover was designed with a centralized checkout system. By the following summer, Woodies converted the Eastover store to a standardized format with new fixtures and individual service desks. On September 29, 1964, a 43,000-square-foot branch opened at the Parole Plaza Shopping Center in Annapolis, Maryland. Unlike

The classic Georgian architecture of the Wheaton store became a design inspiration for future Woodies branches. *Photograph by the author.*

Originally conceived as a self-service budget store, Woodward & Lothrop quickly converted its Eastover location into a full-service branch store in 1964. *Courtesy of the Richard Longstreth Collection.*

Eastover, the Annapolis store carried merchandise that was "traditionally Woodward & Lothrop in quality." Woodies Parole specialized in fashions for men, women, children and gifts for the home. It joined Sears, Britt's, Food Fair and Read's Drug in the regional center. On its opening day, Woodies invited special guests who were given private helicopter flights to view the complex. Over the years, the Parole store grew in size and became a very productive and profitable location for the company.

After the Annapolis store opened, Woodies continued its dramatic growth. After concentrating its last few branches in Maryland, the company returned its focus to Virginia. October 1965 brought Woodward & Lothrop to the new Landmark Shopping Center at Shirley Highway and Duke Street in Alexandria, Virginia. Although it wasn't the largest shopping center in Metropolitan Washington, Landmark Center was the first shopping center on the East Coast with three full-line department stores: Woodies, the Hecht Company and Sears.[63] Woodies called the Landmark location "a blueprint for perfection," as it offered a complete assortment of merchandise at competitive prices and with courteous service. However, Landmark's proximity to the small Alexandria branch added strain to that store's sales levels. Just down the road from Landmark in Springfield, Woodward & Lothrop opened its 450,000-square-foot Shirley Service Building on November 4, 1965. The

The Parole Plaza store in Annapolis, Maryland, soon doubled in size and popularity after its 1964 grand opening. *Courtesy of the Richard Longstreth Collection.*

The Landmark Center store in Alexandria, Virginia, was an early moneymaker for the company after opening in 1965. *Courtesy of the Richard Longstreth Collection.*

Shirley building contained a retail store that offered clearance prices on large articles of furniture, bedding, televisions and appliances. The retail store also offered large stocks of other surplus goods, usually associated with its twice-yearly warehouse sales. Former manager Shirley Mihursky recalls, "People would wait in line starting at 4 a.m. to buy a television. It was mayhem for a day, and it made for a long hard day."

Back in 1963, Woodward & Lothrop purchased the nine-story McLachlen Bank building at Tenth and G Streets NW. The McLachlen building was located adjacent to Woodies' North Building, the former Palais Royal store. When the purchase was announced, a Woodies spokesman said, "At some future date, we plan a complete modernization of our North Building... but we're too busy now on other expansion to work out the North Building details."[64] Historian John DeFerrari recalls, "The North Building had very high ceilings, and Woodies used that as an excuse as to why it couldn't be redeveloped." By 1965, the so-called modernization of the North Building consisted of a plan to raze the structure, along with the newly acquired McLachlen building. In April 1965, Woodward & Lothrop informed a House district subcommittee of its intention to replace the two structures with a new combination department store and office building. A five-story walking bridge would connect the new structure with Woodies' Main Store. The design required congressional approval since Congress had to approve the bridging of any street in Washington.[65] Woodward & Lothrop acknowledged the controversial nature of the design but insisted that it was a vote of confidence in the future of downtown. Many downtown

The aging downtown North Building was targeted for replacement as early as the mid-1960s. *Courtesy of the Richard Longstreth Collection.*

retailers closely followed Woodies' effort to obtain "sky rights" over a street because it signaled new possibilities for downtown construction. The design hit numerous roadblocks, and Woodies eventually put its redevelopment plans on hold and concentrated on further development in the Washington suburbs.

Woodies continued its incredible suburban expansion, but the growth came at the expense of reduced earnings. Annual sales peaked at $100 million, but building expenses grew. That didn't stop Woodward & Lothrop from joining the Hecht Company at the Prince George's Plaza in August 1966. The Plaza Woodies, located on East–West Highway in Hyattsville, Maryland, offered "an excellent quality with easily-affordable prices." Woodward & Lothrop officials saw Prince George's County as a "briskly developing community." The company continued its march into the county with a store at the Iverson Mall in Hillcrest Heights, Maryland. Opened in July 1967, the three-story Iverson Mall Woodies employed a loyal and proud workforce. "We had a great display department [at Iverson]," says manager Shirley Mihursky. "Every morning at Iverson, we would check all of the clothes, and we made sure that the buttons were buttoned and the belts were tied. We took pride in our store." However, in May 1968, after operating a dozen stores throughout the Washington area, Woodward & Lothrop announced the closure of its Bethesda Budget Store and its small Alexandria location. These were the first stores that the company had ever discontinued. The company called both locations profitable, but neither store offered expansion possibilities. Woodies knew that its future was in shopping centers and not in inadequately sized downtown stores. In fact, Bethesda became obsolete as the company began to steer away from budget merchandise, and Alexandria was cannibalized from the nearby Landmark Center Woodies.

In June 1965, Woodward & Lothrop and the Hecht Company announced plans to anchor the Tysons Corner International Shopping Center in Fairfax County, Virginia. The large shopping center was one of the country's largest

The Woodward & Lothrop branch at Prince George's Plaza played an important role in the county's economic development and stability. *Courtesy of the Richard Longstreth Collection.*

The Iverson Mall store was another Prince George's County operation but targeted a more moderate customer base than its Plaza and Montgomery County stores. *Courtesy of the Richard Longstreth Collection.*

Woodies' Tysons Corner store was arguably its most successful and exciting suburban location. Tysons Corner continues to be one of the country's most profitable shopping centers. *Courtesy of the Richard Longstreth Collection.*

This image from November 11, 1977, shows the interior entrance of the Tysons Corner store during one of the store's signature Harvest Sale promotions. *Courtesy of the D.C. Public Library, Washingtoniana Division.*

enclosed malls and opened for business in July 1968. After an initial promise of an anchor spot, Lansburgh's was later denied a location but joined the other anchors in 1969. Tysons Corner became the largest Washington area shopping center, beating out Wheaton Plaza, and annual sales were in excess of $100 million. The mall featured five architecturally sculpted courts, motorized coat racks staffed by philanthropic organizations and the promise of a 4,500-unit International Plaza Apartments complex. It was a much-needed shot in the arm for the department stores since downtown sales had fallen 12 percent over the past year.[66] Donald Godfrey was the first manager at the Tysons Corner Woodward & Lothrop. "I loved it. It had adrenaline, and it had a great staff with good managers," says Godfrey. Former president Edwin Hoffman cites Woodies' success at Tysons on the area's demographics and dense population. Former president Robert J. Mang states, "Tysons was where you made things happen. It was a place where you could work on a project. The energy that you put in at Tysons produced great results." After Tysons opened, Woodward & Lothrop continued to surround Washington with even more suburban locations and engaged in a cat-and-mouse chase with the Hecht Company for market dominance. But before both department stores could concentrate their talents in the suburbs, many Washington retailers needed to tackle major social issues, especially at their downtown stores.

The Sentimental Favorite

Department stores set themselves apart from each other by creating their own identities. Most major American cities contained three types of large stores: one that served the upper-end or "carriage-trade" shopper; one that encompassed all types of merchandise, from its designer salon to its budget basement; and another that catered to shoppers with more moderate means. Washingtonians flocked to Hecht's and Lansburgh's for well-priced staple goods and visited Garfinckel's for merchandise geared toward special occasions. Woodward & Lothrop, on the other hand, carried all types of merchandise for all types of people. It epitomized the classic major American department store. Author Jan Whitaker states that these types of classic stores materialistically defined the American middle-class standard of living: "They brought beauty and pleasure into the lives of a nation of pragmatic, almost stoical people. They provided services to the broad masses that had once been reserved for elites. They became the stewards of the middle class, shaping, cultivating, and enshrining its aspirations and way of life."[67] Broad-reaching stores, such as Woodward & Lothrop, were "places where large numbers of Americans could feel important irrespective of their circumstances," wrote author Richard Longstreth.[68] Woodward & Lothrop bred customer loyalty by offering affordable merchandise that was a little more exclusive than its competition, reasonable credit terms and special events that became part of Washington's culture. "Everything Woodies did, [it] did with class," recalls former employee Shirley Mihursky.

The main floor during one of the downtown store's famous flower shows. *Courtesy of the Historical Society of Washington, D.C.*

Display windows were a very effective and personal form of advertising for major downtown retailers. "A lot of people walked [by] our store every day, and we sold a lot of merchandise from the windows," remembers Waldo Burnside. "We changed the windows every week. The windows played a major role at the downtown store." Windows designer George K. Payne elaborated:

> *The store's management believed that its public thirsted for displays that made the downtown shopping district the place to be. Animated displays became the stuff of family outings, a special occasion for leisure and shopping that reflected the store's identity as a retail institution.*[69]

This was especially true at Christmastime. America's first department store holiday window displays can be traced back to the early 1880s. Most department stores spared no expensive for the holiday season. The grand opening of the Christmas windows marked the official start of holiday buying. All the major stores in Washington hosted elaborate holiday windows, but Woodward & Lothrop always seemed to go one step further with their displays. Waldo Burnside expands on the importance of the window displays: "Christmas windows were rather expensive, but they were important for public relations. And from a practical standpoint, it was a very satisfying experience for the customer."

The first mention of Christmas windows at Woodward & Lothrop appeared in a December 1889 *Washington Post*. These windows told the story of Cinderella and her fairy godmother and contained holiday gift suggestions that "combined the useful with the ornamental."[70] Once inside the store's main floor, customers were greeted by a large display of Santa Claus and his sleigh on an elevated stand. To mark Christmas 1950, Woodies president Andrew Parker traveled to National Airport to greet Santa Claus as he arrived by plane from the North Pole. Santa, while perched on a sleigh, traveled by motorized float into downtown Washington. "Lines of cars followed fore-and-aft with button noses pressed against the window panes. The modern-day Santa arriving by plane, was a new kind of thrill for them," reported the *Washington Post*.[71] His trip ended at Woodward & Lothrop's North Building, where he set up shop and met children and heard their wishes.

Designing the Christmas windows at Woodward & Lothrop was a long process. It took about two years to create the idea, draw up plans and sketches, make figures, develop the mechanization and hold last-minute run-throughs. Windows were traditionally unveiled on Thanksgiving Eve and remained on display until January 2. At one point, Woodies shared its resources with other stores such as Marshall Field, John Wanamaker and B. Altman, and holiday windows traveled to different cities each year to save on costs.

For many years, George K. Payne was the artistic genius behind Woodies' windows. Payne joined Woodward & Lothrop in 1938 and worked his way up to become its display director in 1958. Payne did not just create festively decorated windows; he created a series of elaborate villages, usually historical in nature. Payne felt strongly about the role windows played in the success of the business and in the hearts of customers and their children. One of Payne's most memorable Christmas window themes was entitled "A Window on Williamsburg" and was displayed in 1966. Woodward & Lothrop had a longstanding relationship with the Colonial Williamsburg Foundation, and five thousand visitors a day—a figure that surpasses the combined attendance numbers of all the Smithsonian museum—saw this eight-window exhibit. In Christmas 1956, George Payne helped design a

A young child admires display windows featuring scenes of Christmas in Williamsburg in December 1977. *Courtesy of the D.C. Public Library, Washingtoniana Division.*

A young family enjoys Woodward & Lothrop's elaborate Christmas windows on December 26, 1978. *Courtesy of the D.C. Public Library, Washingtoniana Division.*

On August 2, 1958, officials from the Washington Zoo and Woodward & Lothrop prepare the Eleventh and G Streets NW northwest display window featuring Humboldt penguins, Inca terns and Guanay cormorants. *Courtesy of the D.C. Public Library, Washingtoniana Division.*

A postcard scene of Santa Claus in the store's downtown main floor. *Collection of the author.*

sixty-eight-foot-high Christmas tree on the store's F Street frontage. The massive tree contained over 8,800 twinkling lights and was displayed over the F Street marquee for several holiday seasons. George Payne's talent and responsibilities did not end after the holidays. He was also in charge of interior displays, the sign shop and branch store designs. Payne retired from Woodies in 1970, and Woodward & Lothrop ended its animated holiday windows ten years later.

Woodies' North Building, the former Palais Royal on G Street, was multifunctional. It served as a home store, a housewares center, corporate offices, storage space and special event and exhibit space. The store's Secret Shop was located in the North Building. A staff member accompanied children under twelve into a large sales space where items were priced from twenty-five cents to five dollars. Santa's workshop was appropriately located near the store's toy department. Woodward & Lothrop debuted three new exclusive toys in 1956: Link-It, a construction set of fifty unbreakable pieces; Rub-R-Art, a drawing set that utilized colored rubber bands stretched on plastic pegs; and Play-Doh. Play-Doh was described as a soft molding compound "that does not stain hands, clothing, or the car."[72] Woodies gave Washington, as well as the entire country, its first formal introduction to Play-Doh.

In November 1956, the North Building's second floor housed the traveling show "American Dream Exhibit." Over one thousand historical artifacts were presented to throngs of customers and visitors. Important items included the original Thirteenth Amendment document that outlawed slavery, personal artifacts of President Abraham Lincoln, Babe Ruth's uniform and "better than good watercolors" painted by Adolph Hitler between 1917 and 1919. The Hitler paintings were among the exhibit's most popular displays and "proved two things: that Hitler would have been better off sticking to watercolors, or at least would have been alive, and that the curious take Americana for granted."[73] The exhibits were on loan by individuals and historical societies and were heavily guarded. Many people also recalled that the North Building was the home of the store's Bake Shop. From elaborate cakes to exotic gourmet foods to English Drop Cookies, the Bake Shop was an extremely popular department. English Drop Cookies, also called Woodies' Cookies, were flat, spiced cookies that contained molasses, raisins, nuts, brown sugar and coffee. The recipe for the crackled cookies remains a mystery. The Bake Shop was also popular for its Wellesley Fudge Cupcakes. Waldo Burnside recalls occasional visits to the Bake Shop by a prominent Maryland comptroller:

> *Louis Goldstein was a former comptroller for the state of Maryland.* [Goldstein was one of the longest serving public servants in American history, serving as comptroller from 1959 to 1998.] *Goldstein confessed that whenever he was in Washington, he rode with a state trooper down Eleventh Street and made an illegal U-turn just so he could go into the North Building and purchase a half dozen Wellesley Fudge cupcakes.*

From its Bake Shop to its celebrated holiday traditions, Woodward & Lothrop endeared itself to Washingtonians by going an extra mile with its amenities. "It wasn't the big things that made you great, it was the little things. People paid attention to those little things and that's what made you successful," explains president Waldo Burnside. The federal government acknowledged Woodward & Lothrop's status in the local Washington market. "We even had a relationship with the White House where we helped supply them with china and silver," says former president Robert J. Mang. Media spokesperson Robbie Snow adds, "Whenever something broke at the White House, we were called because we could get it quicker."

In 1930, president Samuel Woodward told a gathering of store employees that he wanted to have "correlating" departments located on the same floor.

The store followed Samuel's direction, and by the 1950s, Woodward & Lothrop acted more as a series of shops, rather than a single large store with massive open spaces filled with all types of merchandise. Internationally renowned commercial designer Raymond Loewy supported this concept and applied it to his future department store designs. "The up-to-date department store is actually a series of specialty or internal shops. When one enters a modern department store, one is no longer confronted with a vast and seething sea of merchandise. Departments have become intimate, dramatic, individual, and personalized," stated Loewy.[74] The shop concept at Woodward & Lothrop was especially prevalent within the women's departments. Most large department stores contained at least one designer salon but Woodies separated each of its apparel departments into its own specially designated shop. In 1965, some of these shops included:

- The Miss Woodward Shop, featuring fashions for the "young elegant"
- The Lady Lothrop Shop, larger-sized women's merchandise showcasing "day and dressy styles"
- The Chandelier Room, containing fine American and European clothing
- The Cosmopolitan Shop, specializing in "after-five" fashions
- The Fashion 5th Shop, featuring fashion-conscious, moderately priced merchandise
- The Top Gear Shop, containing "groovy buys" for juniors
- The Potomac Shop, for clothing "you love to wear now"
- The Plaza III Shop, featuring cocktail, velvet, satin and contemporary dresses

These shops were later followed by:

- The Point of View Shop, carrying "perspective sportswear" made of knits
- The Columbia Sportswear Department, promoting easy-care, comfortable clothing, including pantsuits and knicker suits
- The Scene, featuring electrifying merchandise for juniors

Men's clothing was featured in shops such as the University Shop, for sophisticated young men; Hide and Hair, carrying fur and leather clothing; Quadrangle, for contemporary men's merchandise; and its signature

Woodlothian Collection, featuring classic suits and sportswear. Beginning in 1951, Woodward & Lothrop offered male customers special shopping assistance, even presenting a "stag night" every holiday season. Only male shoppers were allowed into the store for special purchases, shopping aid and an occasional negligee show held in the seventh-floor Tea Room. Woodies' merchandise selections were further expanded when the department store joined the Associated Merchandising Corporation buying group in 1964, after it severed its ties with the Frederick Atkins organization. Over twenty department stores—including Strawbridge & Clothier in Philadelphia, Hutzler's in Baltimore and Hudson's in Detroit—belonged to AMC and enjoyed its large purchasing power. In the 1960s, Woodward & Lothrop began labeling its imported merchandise with special purple tags that indicated "interest and excitement."

Many brides chose Woodward & Lothrop because of its bridal registry and special occasion offerings. Woodies' Wedding Service helped with

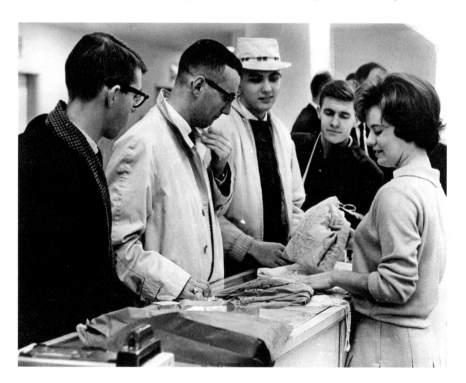

A female employee helps several male customers during one of the store's famous stag night events in December 1962. Men-only stag nights became increasingly popular as the company combined shopping with alcoholic drinks. *Courtesy of the D.C. Public Library, Washingtoniana Division.*

The exterior of the downtown Woodward & Lothrop begins to appear dowdy and dusty during the mid-1970s. *Courtesy of the Richard Longstreth Collection.*

everything from wedding etiquette to china patterns. Consultants recommended wedding gown choices and color schemes for bridal party attendants. The first floor of the downtown store was home to the Silver Room and the Engraving Room, which provided invitations, announcements and any other special paper needs. Woodies stores in downtown Washington, Chevy Chase, Seven Corners and Wheaton Plaza housed Charles of the Ritz Salons that helped brides "look their loveliest." Even after the wedding, Woodward & Lothrop continued to play an important role to new couples. The store's sixth-floor "Ask Mr. Foster" travel service helped the bride and groom with their honeymoon plans, the company's large dry cleaning plant preserved the bride's wedding gown "forever after" and the store's Studio of Interior Decorating helped the new couple settle into their first home "with practical comfort."[75] Woodies' Wedding Bureau kept permanent records of every customer who consulted with the store. "Even husbands have a way of forgetting patterns, you know," said one Wedding Bureau employee. Woodies' popular and large Book Corner helped the young family fill its bookshelves with many of Washington's harder to find titles.

"Woodies was a reliable store that was very conscious of its customers," states former president Robert Mulligan. "We had a good share of the market and we were very profitable." Media spokesperson Robbie Snow notes Woodies' strong customer loyalty. "The major thing that we presented was that we were an independent store [unlike Hecht's and Garfinckel's]," says Snow. "We were the people store, and we were better because we'd been around the longest." Perhaps the allure of Woodward & Lothrop was best summarized in a *Washington Post* article from 1995:

> *Woodies had a bakery. It had dry cleaning. It had a beauty parlor, barber shop and soda fountain. It had hats. It had wedding dresses. It had notions of every kind, and things like ironing board pads and the perfect punch bowl. It had salespeople who became your friends and waited on you year after year...Woodies had cut-glass coasters, Snoopy the Astronaut dolls and Rand McNally official moon maps. It had colonial furniture from the "Williamsburg Shop" or plastic furniture for Young America. It had everything.*[76]

The "Disturbance"

Very few department stores across America were considered "open" to all customers. By the 1930s, many stores established policies, written and/or verbal, for handling trade with African American shoppers. In some of Baltimore's most prominent stores—such as Hutzler's, the May Company and Stewart's—African American customers were only allowed to shop in the downstairs stores. Blacks could be on the main or upper floors only if white customers provided them with a note, granting permission to pick up merchandise on their behalf. In other cities, black customers were not allowed to try on merchandise, especially dresses and hats, and many were followed around the sales floor, their every movement watched. These policies and actions were practiced across the country, not just in the South. Lower-end stores were the exception and tended to be more liberal with their customer base, but discrimination was alive and well in Washington's largest department stores.

One of the earliest printed reports on discrimination in Washington department stores stemmed from an incident in 1919. The *Baltimore Afro American* newspaper reported that all "colored girls" hired during the World War I labor shortage were discharged from Woodward & Lothrop because many white people believed that these employees were overpaid and unable to adequately perform their duties.[77] In 1927, another incident based in Woodward & Lothrop was reported. An angry black shopper complained that a ladies' room was not open to all customers. When she approached the restroom, she was confronted by a "colored maid" and was told that she could no longer enter "THAT one." She was directed to use a lavatory on the sixth floor that was specially designated for colored patrons. The shopper complained to the *Baltimore Afro American*, "I have heard that this store [Woodward & Lothrop] was not especially tickled with their colored trade but they have never been so openly insulting before."[78] In 1939, another black customer wrote to the same paper saying that she was not allowed to take a seat during a public knitting class at Woodward & Lothrop although white shoppers were seated. This action of segregation prompted the insulted black shopper to open her own knitting shop on W Street.

Former media spokesperson Robbie Snow recalls hearing stories of the store's discriminatory practices:

> *I was told that the store had segregated bathrooms that were staffed by black attendants but these attendants could not use these "whites-only" facilities. The "colored" restrooms were very simple. Before our store's 1986 renovation, the old whites-only restroom had a beautiful massive fountain inside the facility. Woodies even had two separate employee entrances.*

In May 1956, several anonymous black employees at Woodward & Lothrop expressed their frustration to the *Washington Afro-American* newspaper. One employee was told by the store's personnel department, "This is a nice place to work. Do as you're told and you will get along all right. We have places for colored and we have places for whites." A maid with fourteen years of service told the paper, "If you are a colored employee here, the highest you'll rise will be the top floor as an elevator operator." Black employees had their own annual celebration for the Twenty Year Club members. While the white employees dined for free at the Statler Hotel and were given their celebratory twenty-dollar check, black workers received five dollars to "buy their own dinner." Complaints to the union were uncommon, as many felt "the union belonged to the company [Woodward & Lothrop]."[79] Company officials stated, "Woodward & Lothrop reserves the right to place employees where it will be in the best interest of the company and will best serve our customers." A Woodies director of public relations addressed the complaints about the segregated employee cafeterias by saying, "Frankly, the colored workers don't have to wait in line as long as whites do to be served in [their] cafeteria."[80] The *Baltimore Afro-American* denounced Woodies' employee restaurant policies. "Jim-Crow conditions exist, despite efforts by the President [Eisenhower] and District commissioners to make Washington a model city of fair play."[81]

A number of department stores were reluctant to open their doors to all patrons for fear that their loyal white clientele base would leave and shop

In 1924, young black men were hired to assist young white children in the store's toy department. Woodward & Lothrop frequently featured live animal displays, especially in its store windows. *Courtesy of the National Photo Company Collection at the Library of Congress.*

elsewhere. Likewise, they discriminated in many of their restaurants and tearooms. African American customers were barred from Woodies' Chevy Chase restaurant. A public relations manager at Woodward & Lothrop declared, "We do not serve Negroes at the Chevy Chase store [restaurant]. No explanation is necessary."[82] When Woodies opened its Wheaton Plaza store on February 5, 1960, several members of the National Association for the Advancement of Colored People (NAACP) picketed the gala celebration. NAACP members urged a boycott of Woodward & Lothrop stores. After a month of picketing and boycott, black shoppers were allowed to eat in the Chevy Chase restaurant. The NAACP called off their protest after the integration of that restaurant.[83]

These types of policies were in no way limited to Woodward & Lothrop. All five of Washington's major retailers engaged in discriminatory practices, especially in regard to hiring. Several civil rights organizations arranged special "no-shopping days" at these stores as a protest. One leader of a group of African American ministers said, "This is not a punitive measure. It is really an instructive one. We want to show them we have purchasing power and get them to see that the Negro wants a better break in employment." In 1961, Woodward & Lothrop began hiring black delivery truck drivers, but drivers noticed that they were assigned to the "worst runs."[84] The Congress of Racial Equality (CORE) played an active role in employee integration. CORE continually pressured Woodies to hire black employees, and in April 1961, four black women, three at the downtown store and one at the Pentagon location, were brought into the company's sales force. Woodward & Lothrop had spurned and defied the CORE's pressure for three years, although the Hecht Company, Lansburgh's and Kann's had already hired black workers. In 1964, CORE organized a long-term public boycott at the downtown Hecht Company store and several of its suburban branches. CORE charged, "Negroes [at Hecht's] with seniority and experience are not promoted to supervisory positions, few Negro women are given permanent sales jobs, and no Negro sales personnel are assigned to 'prestige' or commission departments in the store."[85] In several instances, a token black department store employee was brought out of a stockroom and placed on the sales floor whenever a demonstration occurred.

Department stores became easy targets for demonstrations. Not only did they openly practice segregation and discrimination, they were also high-profile employers in their communities and cities. By the mid-1960s, tensions grew in Washington between police and black citizens during public demonstrations. As the confrontations became more frequent, the gatherings became less orderly. On April 4, 1968, the reverend Dr. Martin Luther King was shot and killed while walking on the balcony of the Lorraine Motel in Memphis, Tennessee. King was an international figure and the nation's leader in the fight for integration. Reverend King fought for civil rights and racial equality through nonviolent protests and demonstrations. His death shocked and angered the nation, and many black citizens in the nation's cities took their grief to the streets. In Washington, a crowd of black citizens assembled at Fourteenth and U Streets shortly after hearing about King's assassination. The crowd asked neighboring businesses to close their doors out of respect for Reverend King and promoted a nonviolent gathering. After a Safeway at Fourteenth and Chapin Streets was broken into and looted, the mood turned angry and destructive.[86] Disturbances grew in several other neighborhoods around North Central Washington, and the commotion began to spread toward the downtown core shopping area. As the crowd made its way down Seventh Street the following day, the Washington police realized that they did not have the manpower to control the looting. Several groups of youths ran through the aisles of Woodward & Lothrop and the

Hecht Company and harassed clerks and snatched merchandise. Store employees quickly boarded the windows and doors and closed their stores. Hundreds of department store employees and customers fled. The exodus clogged the city's streets, and the situation only worsened as other businesses followed the two department stores' lead.[87] Chairman Edwin Hoffman remembers, "We could see that riots were only a block away from the store. It was a very difficult time. There was a lot of uncertainty and unknowns [as to what to do]."

The April 1968 riots could not have come at a worse time for Washington. The city was in the middle of its Cherry Blossom Festival, and tourists turned their attention and their cameras to the damaged shopping area.[88] Mayor Walter E. Washington declared a curfew from 5:30 p.m. to 6:30 a.m. and prohibited the sale of alcoholic beverages, gasoline and other inflammable materials, firearms and ammunition.[89] Thousands of Cherry Blossom Festival attendees fled the city. After three days of burning, looting and demonstrations, Washington became quiet. However, over 645 buildings were damaged during the King riots, half of them determined "unsalvageable." Thirteen thousand National Guard troops arrested 4,352 persons, and medical personnel treated 961 injuries and acknowledged that 6 persons

The downtown Washington Hecht Company store suffered extensive exterior damage during the 1968 riots. *Courtesy of the D.C. Public Library, Washingtoniana Division.*

were killed. A report from the National Planning Commission evaluated the situation that led to the destruction, and many black interviewees complained of being treated poorly by surly white clerks in stores. Certain businesses with a "whites only" cashier employment policy were specifically targeted for looting and retaliation.[90] Interestingly, businesses that were unfamiliar to black shoppers, such as Garfinckel's, were passed over by demonstrators.

Within three months of the April riots, downtown Washington retails plummeted 5 percent. Department stores saw little hope for economic and social improvement in the downtown corridor. Woodward & Lothrop faced severe staff shortages as members of its suburban white female sales force refused to travel into the city. A number of husbands no longer permitted their wives to come downtown to work.[91] Woodies employees and customers suffered frequent harassment by gangs of black youths. The Hecht Company Seventh Street flagship was the target of bomb threats and arson incidents. Increased levels of shoplifting forced Hecht's to hire a significantly larger security staff. The Hecht Company president Edward H. Selonick stated, "The town is behind in urban renewal. Walk along the street and look at the kinds of shops around F Street. It's a beautiful city, but the downtown shopping area is pretty sad."[92]

The riots left Washington, and other cities such as Baltimore, Detroit and Memphis, in shambles but it brought attention to the need for equality. The National Capital Planning Commission emphasized the "pressing need for position action programs" in its May 1968 preliminary report. In 1969, Woodward & Lothrop prominently declared that it was an equal opportunity employer and that it promoted employees on "merit; not race, religion, national origin, or sex."[93] It incorporated black mannequins into its window displays and featured black employees and their accomplishments in the company's in-house *Woodlothian* magazine. "Eventually, black employees were permitted to use any restroom, were paid the same rate as white employees and even used the front door," recalls Robbie Snow.

Unfortunately, many customers perceived the downtown Washington shopping center as dangerous and a magnet for the city's minority shoppers. "The riots finished downtown shopping," says Edwin Hoffman. "Sales dropped off pretty dramatically." Although Garfinckel's was not touched during the April demonstrations, the store remained closed for four days, which resulted in a 1 percent loss of its annual sales. Even prior to the riots, Kann's had suffered sales declines at its downtown location, and the company feared for its future. In 1970, Woodward & Lothrop reported that the 1968 riots had significantly contributed to the downtown store's sales figures' 8- to 10-percent

A quiet day on the main floor of the downtown Woodward & Lothrop on January 23, 1980. Business never fully recovered after the April 1968 riots. *Courtesy of the D.C. Public Library, Washingtoniana Division.*

decline. Many suburban shoppers chose to stay away from the city center and patronize the regional centers. These centers "lacked vehicular congestion, jostling crowds, street noise, the 'wrong' social elements and crime," all qualities associated with downtown Washington.[94] Downtown retailers hoped that a Vietnam War settlement would boost economic and social morale to the city and urban core. However, the first casualty of Washington's troubled and battered downtown was Lansburgh's. The company was never able to regain its economic footing, and its owner, City Stores Corporation, was impatient. City Stores not only closed the downtown store in 1973, it closed the entire division, including a two-month-old location at the Springfield Mall. Some branches were sold to E.J. Korvette, and one in Rockville, Maryland, operated for seven months as Lit Brothers, a City Stores department store from Philadelphia. City Stores executive vice-president Louis G. Melchior stated that its Seventh Street location was battered from a difficult shopping environment. Upon Lansburgh's closure in mid-1973, Melchior reminded the *Washington Post*, "The downtown Lansburgh's never fully recovered from— what do you call it?—the Disturbance."[95]

Exact Change

B y the late 1960s, the department store industry, along with America's social and economic norms, was rapidly changing. Department stores realized that their futures were in the suburbs and their aging overbuilt flagships were liabilities. They were expensive to maintain, and suburban expansions and competitions eroded their profitability. It was clear that many of the older stores were worth more for their real estate than as ongoing business. Price and convenience were more valuable than loyalty and familiarity. Department stores, in Washington and across the country, made some tough decisions. "People do not like change, but change is a necessity in order to survive," states executive vice-president Howard Lehrer. Former chairman Edwin Hoffman agrees, "For sentimentality reasons, a community does not like change."

Though it was still the Washington market leader, Woodward & Lothrop worked at a severe disadvantage when compared to its peer retailers. The Hecht Company was funded by the May Company; Garfinckel's was part of a new conglomerate that included Brooks Brothers and Miller & Rhoads; and Lansburgh's was a unit of City Stores Corporation. Even Kann's, the smallest of the lot, was owned by L.S. Good Co. from Wheeling, West Virginia. All these stores relied on their out-of-town owners for expansion expenses and help during temporary sales declines. Woodward & Lothrop was Washington owned and Washington managed. The company was a retail anomaly as more and more department stores either successfully merged with a parent company or simply closed their doors. In January

Back in the 1950s, most of Woodies' merchandise on its main floor was kept behind counters. This image shows the store's familiar clock and F Street doors. *Courtesy of the D.C. Public Library, Washingtoniana Division.*

1967, Woodward & Lothrop announced that it had entered into merger negotiations with the Dayton Co., a Minneapolis department store chain. Both businesses were family owned and were looking to expand. At the time of the talks, Woodward & Lothrop operated twelve department stores while Dayton's consisted of six full-line department stores and seven company-owned Target discount stores. The combined corporation would potentially post annual sales of over $300 million. Two weeks after the announcement, the merger plan was dissolved. Inside reports stated that both sides could not agree on a management philosophy.[96] One year later, Dayton's engaged in a successful merger with the mammoth J.L. Hudson Company of Detroit. The combined stores formed the Dayton Hudson Corporation, the forerunner to the Target Corporation.

One of the biggest changes in the Woodward & Lothrop's history was the sudden resignation of president and CEO Andrew Parker on August 8, 1969. Parker was the third generation of founder Samuel Walter Woodward, and none of Parker's children was involved in the business. Parker became store president in 1947 and chief executive officer in 1964. He oversaw the company's suburban expansion into a twelve-store organization and led the company through many of the economic and social changes that affected the downtown Washington store. Woodward & Lothrop's board of directors accepted Parker's immediate resignation "with great regret." At the time of the resignation, Parker stated, "I merely feel that it's in the best interest of the corporation and myself that a change be made."[97] He expressed an interest in spending more time on civic and charitable projects and continued to serve on Woodies' board as vice-chairman. Lotie (Lothrop) Luttrell remained with the company as the chairman of the executive committee, but he was not involved in the store's merchandising. "Lotie was farther removed from the store," stated buyer Donald Godfrey. Andrew Parker recommended that Edwin K. Hoffman, vice-president and general manager, become the next president and CEO, and the company's board of directors approved the nomination.

Edwin Hoffman was no stranger to American retailing. Before his arrival in Washington, Hoffman served as president of Cleveland's Higbee Co. department store and Philadelphia's iconic John Wanamaker. He joined Higbee's in 1955 and became its president in 1962. In 1967, he assumed the title of Wanamaker's president and chief executive. Wanamaker's was a beloved Philadelphia institution that was steeped in tradition. Its Center City Philadelphia flagship contained an interior multistory Grand Court that was home to a two-ton bronze eagle and the

John Wanamaker was a Philadelphia institution that shared many of the same business principles as Woodward & Lothrop. Throughout the years, many parallels were made between the two businesses. The final parallel was made in 1987 when Woodward & Lothrop purchased the John Wanamaker stores. *Collection of the author.*

world's largest pipe organ. But by the 1960s, John Wanamaker began to lose its luster, and many of its stores became dowdy and dated. Wanamaker's continually lost market share in Philadelphia to competitors such as Strawbridge & Clothier and Bamberger's. Hoffman and Wanamaker's were a terrible match. Hoffman recalls his tenure in Philadelphia:

> *I never should have gone to Wanamaker's. It was the worst store in the country. The merchandise was thirty years old. They changed nothing. It was an awful store. I couldn't believe the shape that it was in when I got there. I didn't fit in there at all, and it troubled me.*

Hoffman wanted to make significant changes at Wanamaker's, but the company's board of directors protested Hoffman's plans for the store. About fifteen months into his presidency of the department store, Hoffman and Wanamaker parted ways. "As Sinatra sang, 'I did it my way.' They fired me, thank God," said Hoffman.

Over the next two decades, Edwin Hoffman was one of the most visible and colorful figures of Woodward & Lothrop. He was just as active with the Board of Trade as he was with the Kennedy Center. Some members of the founding families were skeptical of Hoffman's intentions. "After Wanamaker's fired him, Ed Hoffman was on his way south to take a break. He stopped by Woodies and talked to us. Much to my dismay my father [Andrew Parker] asked him, 'Why don't you come work with us?'" says Brainard Parker. After Andrew stepped down, Brainard and other family members held Hoffman fully responsible for all company actions, while former store vice-chairman Robert Mulligan criticized the family's lack of involvement in the store management: "They saw Woodies as their candy store, and they just saw it as their inheritance." Regardless of the internal dynamics, Hoffman continued the company's expansion program and worked hard to keep the stores profitable.

In spring 1969, Allan Bloostein arrived at the Hecht Company and brought new life to that department store chain. With the financial and institutional support of its parent, the May Company, Bloostein quietly transformed the sleepy, moderately priced store into a modernized business that reached out to younger shoppers with new fashionable merchandise while maintaining its traditional clientele.[98] By 1970, the Hecht Company was a very close second to Woodward & Lothrop in sales. Woodies retaliated by launching a full renovation of the Main Building downtown. Vice-president John Israelson told the *Washington Post*, "Strengthening of this store is an indication of our optimism for the downtown of this city. Someone has to start it."[99] In hindsight, Woodies executive vice-president Howard Lehrer reflects, "[During the 1970s] Hecht's upgraded very selectively and with thought behind it. Woodies [and its merchandise] just stood still."

In August 1971, Woodies opened a location in the "new city" of Columbia, Maryland. A development of the Rouse Corporation, Columbia was America's first planned community and was located midway between Washington and Baltimore. In 1967, the first families settled in Columbia, and by 1971, its population was over twenty thousand with five hundred people moving into the community each month.[100] Woodies "patterned the [Columbia] store on the European retail separation of departments and was reminiscent of the main store of Bloomingdales." The Columbia Mall was designed to include five anchor department stores. Woodward & Lothrop opened during the mall's first phase along with Baltimore's Hochschild, Kohn. Woodies proved to be much more successful in Columbia than Hochschild's. "[Woodies] advertised like crazy in the *Washington Post*, and most people in Columbia got the *Washington Post*," says department store buyer Don Alexander. The company heavily utilized its famous jingle, "Make your world beautiful at Woodies!" In May 1972, Woodward & Lothrop continued its expansion plans and opened a location in Landover, Maryland. Landover Mall was hailed as a "much needed economic and psychological boost for Prince George's County."[101] The county contained a number of economically stable middle-class citizens, but it was better known as a less-affluent, predominantly black community. Many Washington retailers had shunned Prince George's County, and Landover was the first mall in the Washington area that included four

Woodward & Lothrop opened a store in the "new" Maryland city of Columbia on August 2, 1971. Many of the city's earliest residents were transplanted from the immediate Washington area and were longtime loyal Woodward & Lothrop shoppers. *Courtesy of the Richard Longstreth Collection.*

department stores under one roof. It was Woodies' twelfth store, and the company advertised, "Woodies...better by the dozen." The initial success of Landover came at the expense of the company's small Eastover Shopping Center store, also located in Prince George's County. The store closed only one month after the Landover opening. Eastover never met the company's expectations. "We had to merchandise it in a different way," says Waldo Burnside. "Eastover was at the bottom of our stores, and as a group, we were slow to close some stores."

After Landover's opening, analysts encouraged Woodward & Lothrop to look beyond its immediate Washington trading area and specifically explore the corridor from northern Baltimore down to Richmond. But Waldo Burnside knew that Richmond was Thalhimers territory. "Billy Thalhimer

Landover Mall, in Prince George's County, was the first Washington-area enclosed mall that contained four anchor stores: Sears, Hecht Company, Woodward & Lothrop and Garfinckel's. The mall opened in May 1972. *Courtesy of the Richard Longstreth Collection.*

Woodies' long-delayed Montgomery Mall store finally opened for business in March 1976. A dispute over land rights and sewage issues delayed the store's opening for almost nine years. *Courtesy of the Richard Longstreth Collection.*

was a legend in his own time. He was the perfect person to run a Southern store." Instead, Woodies announced in 1967 that it would move into a new large enclosed shopping center in Maryland's Montgomery County. The Montgomery Mall opened in 1968, but due to a sewer moratorium, Woodies' move was delayed for years. Woodward & Lothrop finally opened on March 25, 1976. Three thousand customers jammed into the store during its first two hours on opening day. A spokesman said, "The bright picture at the Washington company makes it one of the leaders among retailers nationally in terms of percentage growth." The store carried more high-end contemporary designer merchandise than most of its other locations. Noticeably absent was a major appliance department, but with the store's emphasis on better fashions and home goods, Woodies felt that the Montgomery store was well positioned to strengthen its image in the Washington market. However, in many ways, Woodies' Montgomery store faced its stiffest challenge from its sister store at Tysons Corner. "Montgomery never really took off because Tysons was just across the river and offered better options," says Robert Mang.

Poor parking and additional competition from a new neighboring Neiman Marcus store hindered the success of the Chevy Chase Woodward & Lothrop's. Woodies considered building a large shopping complex in a different location and attaching a new store. But these expansion plans were hampered by zoning restrictions that played in and out of the courts for many years. In the end, the Chevy Chase store was never truly altered or relocated, yet it remained a reasonably successful branch. Some executives saw the moderate success at Chevy Chase as a lost opportunity. "We didn't have the money to do with Chevy Chase what we should have. It was an old physical plant that needed to be remodeled," says executive vice-president Howard Lehrer.

The mid-1970s brought some major changes and challenges to Woodward & Lothrop. In 1973, Thalhimers of Richmond became the first major department store in the country that allowed shoppers to use a Master Charge for store purchases, along with its own store charge.[102] This created a big uproar within the department store industry, as retailers depended on store charge programs for profitability and loyalty. However, the controversial move at Thalhimers profited sales. Purchases by customers who chose not to open store accounts and out-of-town shoppers increased. In 1974, Garfinckel's became the first large Washington retailer to accept bank credit cards. Woodward & Lothrop followed suit in March 1976. Woodies vice-president of marketing said,

Left: An image of the Eleventh and G Streets NW corner of the downtown store. This corner became the location of the busy Metro Center subway station in 1976. *Courtesy of the Historic American Buildings Survey at the Library of Congress.*

Below: An early view of the rear parking lot at Woodies' Chevy Chase store. Within a few years of the Chevy Chase store's opening, the parking lot was clearly too small for the amount of business that the location received. *Courtesy of the Richard Longstreth Collection.*

A photograph of Woodies' direct entrance into its downtown store from the Metro Center subway station. The busy entryway opened directly into a new bakery and prepared-food department. *Photograph by the author.*

"the bicentennial was the main reason for breaking with a department store tradition of handling its own credit."[103]

As visitors flocked to Washington for the bicentennial celebration, they were greeted by the city's new Metro subway system. The Metro opened on March 27, 1976, eleven years after Congress authorized its construction. At the time of its opening, it was the most expensive transit system in the world. Some Washingtonians dubbed the subway construction "the greatest non-riotous disruption to Washington urban life."[104] As the only store with a direct subway entrance, Woodies had a great advantage. The subway station "Metro Center" brought throngs of shoppers into the downtown store, but this advantage came with a price. The department store relinquished its tunnel under G Street that connected the Main Store with the North Building. By 1976, the bakery moved to the Main Store while the Food Shop remained in the North Building. "Instead of bread moving by handcart 100 yards through the tunnel, it will be trucked five blocks due to street patterns there," said a Woodies spokesperson.[105] In addition, Woodies' basement, home to the company's Budget Shop, lost a sizeable share of floor space in order to accommodate the new entrance.

As Woodies grappled with a fresh fashionable image in the face of new competition, the store reevaluated its budget departments throughout the entire chain, especially downtown. In response, Woodies decided to abandon a separate budget shop and integrated the merchandise into the upper floors. The department store insisted that its customer base wanted to trade up. Former vice-chairman Robert Mulligan agrees about the necessity of removing the Budget Shop: "That's not what we wanted the traffic from the Metro entrance to see first." One out of every four Woodies customers entered the store through its subway entrance.[106] A new "Metro level" that included juniors' departments and food stalls replaced the budget store.

A display window at the Chevy Chase store displays the disastrous new company logo from 1978. The "updated" logo was abandoned after only eight months. *Photograph by the author.*

Woodward & Lothrop also made changes to the company name in an effort to present a more aggressive and innovative image. The once sleepy Washington market was becoming crowded and competitive, and Woodies executives thought that a new progressive logo, in addition to the new merchandise, would help protect its perception as the city's fashion leader. In July 1978, the company began advertising itself as Woodward/Lothrop. The new name incorporated a new font with solid *O*s. It was an attempt to portray Woodies as a "more fashionable, more contemporary" store. Loyal customers were outraged by the change. Some complained that the solid *O*s "looked like what children do in comic books." Store officials were frustrated by the negative responses. "The longer the *O*s were kept filled, the worse the store's image would become," said one executive. Many customers simply did not want filled-in *O*s and a slash instead of an ampersand. They wanted "Good Old Woodies." After investing two years of planning alongside a six-figure development cost, Woodward & Lothrop abandoned the logo change after only eight months.[107]

A. Lothrop "Lotie" Luttrell retired as Woodies' chairman of the board in May 1978. Lotie was the last of the Lothrop family line involved in the store's management. He remained as a board director, along with Andrew Parker, but Edwin Hoffman succeeded Lotie as chairman of Woodies' board of directors. Waldo Burnside, a longtime Woodies employee and executive vice-president, was promoted to president of Woodward & Lothrop.

Stores that were headquartered in other cities began to infiltrate the Washington metropolitan area in the 1970s. The biggest threat was Bloomingdale's. In 1977, Bloomingale's, "New York's citadel of consumption," opened its first full-line store at the Tysons Corner shopping center in Virginia. Located in the former Lansburgh's store, Bloomingdale's also announced another location at the White Flint Mall in Rockville, Maryland. Bloomingdale's promised to take on "all the fine [Washington] stores." Woodward & Lothrop found itself being attacked on both ends. Hecht's was stronger in merchandise and price points while Bloomingdale's, along with Lord & Taylor, provided better upper-end designer offerings. Ed Hoffman decided that Woodies needed to be a "fashion right store." "We [Woodward & Lothrop] had to get sharper, quicker," recalls Hoffman. "We were losing a lot of market share. They were carving the hell out of a marketplace that used to be ours." Woodies took the new competition very seriously. President Robert Mang agreed that a fashion-oriented merchandise mix would bring more traffic into the store. "[In the 1970s] Washington became a major opportunity town," says Mang. "We didn't give up providing good customer service, and we stayed close to the community. But customers love something new." Waldo Burnside agreed, "A lot of older [Washington] stores came from a very long tradition. They stocked their stores with what made them famous, and then they didn't adjust."

In the late 1970s, Woodward & Lothrop felt that additional suburban stores in Washington could stall outsiders such as Bloomingdale's, Neiman-Marcus, Saks Fifth Avenue and I. Magnin. Woodies agreed to open in two new shopping malls designed by Michigan real estate entrepreneur A. Alfred Taubman. Taubman was a well-known and successful shopping center developer, and he planned two new Washington-area malls: Lake Forest in Gaithersburg, Maryland, and Fair Oaks in Fairfax County, Virginia. Both malls were constructed far from the immediate Washington metropolitan region, located in areas that preceded residential development. Taubman tended to rapidly open large shopping malls in undeveloped areas and then wait a few years for the area to populate. Lake Forest in Gaithersburg opened in September 1978. It struggled to develop an audience and was

The interior entrance to the Montgomery Mall branch location. The logo featuring the "hooked O's" was popular for many years. *Photograph by the author.*

slow to fill store vacancies. The same was true two years later at Fair Oaks. It was the wrong time for retail expansion as the country found itself in an economic recession. "Taubman was a lot like other developers who thought that they knew the retail business. The Taubman Company thought that if it put its foot on the accelerator [and built more centers], it would create more profit," says Walter Burnside. Ed Hoffman trusted Taubman's judgment and remained committed to both malls. As Woodward & Lothrop approached its one hundredth anniversary, the department store wanted to be optimistic about its second century.

One Hundred Years Old

[Woodward & Lothrop] *is an integral part of our community…a great business, civic organization, not just selling merchandise. Woodies has a surplus and we* [the city] *don't.*[108]
—*Mayor Marion Barry Jr.*
February 28, 1980
Woodward & Lothrop's one-hundredth-birthday celebration.

The 1980s was arguably the most eventful decade in Woodies' history. The company projected an image as Washington's number one retailer, in spite of the new out-of-town competition that entered the market. "People enjoyed coming to work [at Woodies] every day because we were winning," says vice-president David Mullen. "We were still taking market share. Maximizing bestselling merchandise was what our success and strategy was all about," states Mullen. Woodward & Lothrop threw a lavish one-hundredth-birthday celebration on February 28, 1980. Held in the Capital Hilton ballroom, the gala was attended by many of Washington's political and social leaders. *Washington Post* chairwoman Katharine Graham spoke, "[Woodies] is a whale of a business success story, and it is obviously run by a very brilliant and able management team." Columnist Art Buchwald quipped, "Washington would be just another small town surrounded by Bloomindale's [if it weren't for Woodies]."[109] With annual sales at an all time high, the department store seemed poised to enter the 1980s with confidence and optimism.

Chairman Ed Hoffman led the charge of upgrading the store's position in the Washington marketplace. By the early 1980s, the store had dropped

Woodward & Lothrop entered the immediate Baltimore area in 1981 with a store at the White Marsh Mall. The store, located about ten miles north of downtown, consistently failed to meet sales expectations. *Courtesy of the Richard Longstreth Collection.*

The White Marsh Woodies was located in one of James Rouse's signature shopping center properties. *Photograph by the author.*

its budget stores and hard line goods such as large appliances. Hoffman's strategy was to make Woodward & Lothrop a fashion-oriented retailer, not just Washington's traditional all-purpose department store. Hoffman told the *Washington Post*, "We don't like being called a department store anymore. It makes us sound old and stodgy, and we don't think we are." He referred to the store as "a quick and major purveyor of merchandise, [particularly] to people in upper-income brackets."[110] For years, Woodward & Lothrop wanted to expand its customer base and considered the Frederick, Maryland, and Hampton Roads, Virginia, marketplaces. The company successfully established a loyal customer base with its Columbia and Annapolis stores. The Baltimore area was the next likely and reasonable move for company expansion. Hutzler's operated Baltimore's highest-grossing department store in the northern suburb of Towson, and Hecht's and Hochschild's were either building or operating profitable stores in the Towson market. Although unsuccessful at establishing a Towson presence, Woodward & Lothrop settled on a location in the new White Marsh Mall in northeast Baltimore County. Located right off of Interstate 95, White Marsh was built by the Rouse Corporation and featured five department stores, including Hutzler's, JCPenney, Sears and Bamberger's, the Newark, New Jersey–based powerhouse operated since 1929 by R.H. Macy Co. By the mid-1970s, Baltimore-based Hutzler's had begun its downward spiral in the Baltimore market, and its new White Marsh store did not command attention. Instead, the attention was focused on Bamberger's. Woodward & Lothrop felt confident competing with Bamberger's. "We had more fruit cocktail and icing on the cake than Bamberger's. We were a step above," says buyer Donald Godfrey. "Bamberger's was going after the belly of the customer. We [Woodies] carried a lot of better merchandise in addition to the standard lines."

However, Woodies' results at White Marsh were mixed, and sales figures did not meet company projections. "White Marsh had a good management team but its customer was not ready for us," says Godfrey. The company also attributed some of its struggles to the mall's location. "It was located just a little ahead of the [Baltimore] market," says president Robert Mang. "It was a little far north before the population got to it." After the White Marsh store opened to lackluster results, Woodward & Lothrop curtailed its ambitious expansion plans.

Woodward & Lothrop was not the only Washington store that experienced changes during the 1980s. Garfinckel's, once the area's premiere high-fashion retailer, was purchased by the Allied Stores Corporation in September

1981. Since 1967, Garfinckel operated Brooks Brothers, Ann Taylor, Miller & Rhoads and numerous other well-known stores. Allied's purchase of the entire Garfinckel organization was not solicited; it was a hostile takeover, one that would typify many of the mergers and closures that wreaked havoc throughout the retail world. Allied Stores Corporation was an experienced department store holding company, but Washington's Garfinckel's stores were considered specialty stores. Allied did not have experience running high-fashion divisions, and the Washington Garfinckel stores needed support and direction. Stores such as Saks Fifth Avenue, Neiman-Marcus and I. Magnin chipped away at its market, and shoppers were drawn to these newer stores. Garfinckel's locations became dowdy and dated. One former Woodies executive commented, "Garfinckel's was living on an image. In Washington, you have to be where the people are, and the Washington area is full of middle income people."

The situation was different at the Hecht Company. One former Woodward & Lothrop executive felt that Hecht's took advantage of some of Woodies' missteps. He stated, "Hecht's muscled in behind to snatch the middle-market shoppers who were confused by Woodies' message; once they'd started to shop at Hecht's, they rarely returned to Woodies." Hecht's offered brand-name merchandise, decent service, energized store environments and a complete selection of goods. It was a promotional store that featured frequent sales and discount coupons. Woodies president Robert Mang says, "Woodies developed good relationships with its vendors and was very customer oriented. But we weren't the 'bang away' lowest price store, and Woodies had to become significantly more promotional [in order to address Hecht's sales advances]." Woodward & Lothrop had an advantage downtown with a sizeable store located above Washington's busiest subway station, Metro Center. Hecht's downtown store still operated out of its outdated building on Seventh Street. Historian John DeFerrari recalls the downtown Hecht's during the early 1980s: "Hecht's at Seventh and F Streets was dingy looking. It was limping along, very drab. The help looked like they didn't want to be there." Woodies president Edwin Hoffman agrees: "Hecht's was a dinosaur. It was an old property that required a lot of maintenance. It was incredibly expensive to operate." Hecht's wanted a new store, and it wanted to be near Metro Center. The company threatened to leave downtown altogether. In May 1983, Washington's Redevelopment Land Agency agreed to allow the sale and development of a new Hecht's store at Twelfth and G Streets NW. Woodies welcomed Hecht's relocation, but it was a mixed blessing. The two department stores created a new compact downtown shopping center accessible by the city's increasingly popular subway system. Customer foot traffic increased, but sales competition intensified.

Even with newcomers entering the market and competitors, such as Hecht's, strengthening their merchandise, Woodward & Lothrop felt confident of its status in the Washington community. "[In the early 1980s] Woodies had no problems with its future," says a former executive. "Every year was a good year, and we never had a bad month. We were taking market share from everyone." Industry sales figures assured Woodward & Lothrop that it was "crushing" Bloomingdale's in the Washington market. The picture was seemingly perfect at Woodies until December 1983. Investor Ronald Baron, president of Baron Capital, Inc., approached Edwin Hoffman and informed Hoffman that he and his clients owned almost 20 percent of the company stock. At the time, Woodies' stock was trading for about fifty dollars a share, and Baron asked Hoffman if he was interested in buying his shares for sixty dollars a share. Hoffman was infuriated. If he didn't accept Baron's offer, Hoffman risked losing the company and his chairmanship. Woodward & Lothrop was not the only department store that Baron targeted for a takeover. Family-run Strawbridge & Clothier in Philadelphia also received unsolicited offers of purchase. Baron said that he was interested in these stores because "there aren't many independent retailers left in the country. They are attractive takeover candidates because, if someone else wants to get into a market, it is far easier to buy existing stores than to start them up."[111] Woodies' board of directors did everything they could to block the purchase and even refused to release financial documents to Baron. The board decided that it had to find its own buyer in order to protect the company's assets and investments—and the sooner, the better. "We were public, and we were in play," says vice-chairman Robert Mulligan. "We had to do something."

Just five months after Baron approached Woodies about its takeover attempt, Ed Hoffman and his board found a buyer for the department store. Developer A. Alfred Taubman, owner of Washington's Fair Oaks and Lakeforest Malls among many others throughout the country, offered to purchase Woodies for $200 million. "Al [Taubman] and I went way back, and we had a mutual respect," says Ed Hoffman. The board of directors quickly accepted the purchase, but it still required approval by Woodies' shareholders. Members of the Woodward and Lothrop families held large amounts of company stock and were upset and angry over the quick pace of the company's purchase. Some store officials were supportive of the sale but also felt that Hoffman and Taubman didn't treat the family members well.

A feud developed between family members and company management. Woodward family member Brainard Parker recalls, "I have bitter recollections of Taubman and Hoffman hoodwinking. I'm hostile. They were selfish people who took what they could." The situation even strained family relations. "My father and brother were estranged because of the sale. But my father [former president and board vice-chairman Andrew Parker] felt that he had done the right thing by siding with Hoffman. He decided that he had put enough time into Woodies." Management complained that surviving family members were never involved in the business, but "when it became time to sell, they became experts." Skeptical shareholders were convinced that the only reason Taubman was interested in purchasing the store was for its valuable real estate. "Taubman knew the value of real estate really well and Woodward & Lothrop owned a lot of real estate and long-term leases," said Lothrop family member Nathaniel Orme. Looking back, Ed Hoffman believes that "the families felt deeply about the company, and they worried what would happen if they were out. It was a Washington institution, and they wanted to keep it that way." Both management officials and family members played out their disagreements in the press. Taubman's offer required an immediate response. Woodward & Lothrop's family members went to court to fight the company's purchase by Taubman. They argued that the board was orchestrating its own takeover and sought "their own White Knight." Hoffman shrugged off their only prospect, Monroe G. Milstein, founder of Burlington Coat Factory Warehouse. Although Milstein promised a higher per share amount, the feasibility of his offer never materialized. By December, the courtroom battle ended. Taubman raised his purchase price offer to $227.5 million and agreed to pay the family $2 million in courtroom legal costs. The outstanding shareholders dropped their litigation against Taubman. Even though all parties finally agreed to the store's acquisition, Brainard Parker feels that "there would still be a Woodward & Lothrop if it weren't [for Hoffman and Taubman]."

For years, the department store had wanted to replace its aging North Building, the old Palais Royal. The company wanted to redevelop the site back in the 1960s, but its plans were strongly opposed by zoning officials. Through the 1970s, Woodies exerted little effort to modernize the structure and simply held on to the real estate for excess sales space and certain corporate offices. Located almost adjacent to the 1983 Washington Convention Center, the land was valuable. Woodward & Lothrop was anxious to facilitate the development of a mixed-use project that included offices, parking and a luxury hotel. It would provide a beneficial connection

By the early 1980s, Woodies' North Building, the former Palais Royal, became outmoded and outdated. The company pleaded to historic committees to allow for its demolition. Woodward & Lothrop did not fully vacate the property until February 1987. *Courtesy of the Richard Longstreth Collection.*

between the Woodies store and the proposed Convention Center. By the time the Convention Center opened, historical preservation groups opposed its demolition. Woodward & Lothrop insisted that its North Building was "too structurally unsound for further renovation." The D.C. Historic Preservation Review protested since the North Building was one of the city's only remaining examples of the Chicago School style of commercial architecture.

In 1978, the District of Columbia enacted the Historic Landmark and Historic District Protection Act (D.C. law 2-144). This was designed to protect and safeguard historic landmarks while "fostering civic pride in accomplishments of the past." The act also encouraged finding alternative uses for existing historic structures rather than demolishing aging properties for other purposes. With the cooperation of the mayor's office, a historic structure could be demolished if a proposed project proved that it offered "special merit." Mayor Marion Barry sent the demolition request to the district's office of compliance in the district's Department of Consumer and Regulatory Affairs, as directed by preservation law. The department director determined that redevelopment of the Woodies North Building proved "special merit" as the developer demonstrated that the building's rehabilitation was impractical and impossible. The office determined that the North Building demolition was "probably the strongest special-merit case we [District of Columbia] have had yet." Members of the nonprofit D.C. Preservation League protested the demolition plan, especially after the D.C. Historic Preservation Review Board recommended its protection. However, the Preservation League dropped its protests after its membership felt that the district's decision would be unlikely to be overturned.[112] In preparation for the building's closure, Taubman moved most of the company's support staff to a new office building in Alexandria, Virginia, near Telegraph Road and the Washington Beltway. Woodies did not fully empty the North Building until February 1987.

By 1985, Woodward & Lothrop was no longer a locally owned Washington institution. To pay off the massive debt, Al Taubman needed the company to perform well. He promised not to change the company's identity, yet he felt that higher-end merchandise would give Woodies a better image along with greater sales and profits. He directed the company to integrate higher-priced goods into the stores. "The thing that made Woodward & Lothrop great was its merchandise mix," says a former employee. "Taubman didn't understand the [merchandise mix]. Our best stores were in downtown and in Chevy Chase, but he wanted the same upper-end goods in Lake Forest [a Taubman mall]. There was no way it was going to work." Taubman was not a merchant, and his misunderstanding of the store's trading ability was disastrous to the department store. One former Woodies buyer states, "Woodies' problems began when they started presenting goods that they thought people should be buying as opposed to what they wanted to buy. Stores can't tell customers what they're supposed to want. It'll screw up your customers. They feel beaten up and go someplace else."

On October 31, 1985, the Hecht Company opened its new $40 million flagship department store at Twelfth and G Streets NW. Over thirty-five thousand people visited the store on opening day and prompted fire officials to close the doors intermittently for safety reasons. For much of the past decade, Hecht's had been slowly upgrading and updating its suburban stores. The new flagship gave the company the opportunity to "polish its image" at a very visible location. Hecht's aging Seventh Street store closed two days before the Twelfth Street location's opening. That closing gave the company the chance to display new merchandise that wasn't geared exclusively to budget-minded shoppers. The merchandise at the new

The Chevy Chase Woodward & Lothrop was consistently a profitable and popular performer. However, by the 1980s, the building became dated in its appearance, especially in contrast with the adjacent new Mazza Gallerie shopping complex. *Photograph by the author*.

An interior photo of the Chevy Chase Woodward & Lothrop store in the early 1990s. *Photograph by the author*.

A reinvented Hecht's store became a Metro Center neighbor to the downtown Woodward & Lothrop store in October 1985. The new Hecht flagship brought excitement and competition to the immediate shopping area. *Photograph by the author.*

downtown Hecht's store was now more in line with the assortment offered at Woodies than what was previously offered at its former F Street flagship. The new relocated Hecht's store gave hope that the city's downtown was finally "overcoming years of decay and neglect." The *Washington Post* praised the new addition to downtown.

"Austere and dignified, strong if staid, the new Hecht's Metro Center department store stands amid the ruins of G Street, promising better days to come. Its architecture speaks quietly to the street, commanding attention by its presence without unseemly shouts," the *Post* reported. However, the newspaper also commented on the changing look of department store interiors. "Older department stores like Hecht's Seventh Street landmark, with their lofty, ornately columned ceilings, made shopping seem as exciting as going to the Opera House in Vienna. This store seems more business than theater."[113]

In addition to Hecht's downtown rebirth, competition strengthened when Macy's and Nordstrom publicly expressed interest in the Washington market. One retail analyst commented to the *Washington Post*, "If I were in either Woodward & Lothrop's or The Hecht Co.'s shoes, I would be very nervous."[114] Woodward & Lothrop felt confident that its longtime role in the Washington retail scene would secure its rightful place as market leader. "Woodies was a Washington institution, and we weren't part of the government; we were a business," says media spokesperson Robbie Snow.

In 1984, the company embarked on a $20 million renovation of its downtown Washington flagship store. As historian John DeFerrari comments, Woodies appeared "old and creaky." Famed architect Michael Graves supervised the building's transformation. Company officials called it "the most extensive renovation in the company's history." Washington architecture and art critic Ben Forgey praised Michael Graves's involvement in the project. "That an architect of Graves's behemoth reputation was selected for so straightforward a restoration job is due in large measure to Graves's previous work for Taubman," said Forgey.[115] The main floor received extra attention as the ceilings were lowered, new chandeliers were installed and floors were retiled with marble from Italy and Tennessee. The floor featured fashion excitement, where "beautiful traditions are renewed

The corner of Eleventh and F Streets NW as it appeared in the early 1990s. *Photograph by the author.*

The G Street entrance to the downtown Woodward & Lothrop store as it appeared in the early 1990s. *Photograph by the author.*

with forward-looking spirit, wit, and eye-filling richness," according to the store's publicity. On October 20, 1986, Woodies held a gala reopening event that benefitted the Kennedy Center and the National Symphony Orchestra. "That was my baby," says Ed Hoffman about Woodies' 1986 renovation. "We cleaned up the store because we had to be competitive." However, John DeFerrari called it a "very restrained face lift."[116] He continued, "Woodies was not a restoration, it was a refurbishment. They just kind of cleaned it up, painted it and brought out its historic sense." At its grand reopening, over four hundred employees, each holding three helium balloons, formed a human chain around the building. It was a grand event and another sign of downtown Washington's rebirth as a shopping destination. The future appeared good for Woodies. Within two weeks, Taubman announced the purchase of Philadelphia's John Wanamaker stores. The company quickly doubled in size but also doubled its problems.

Double Trouble

On November 4, 1986, A. Alfred Taubman announced his $183 million purchase of Philadelphia's John Wanamaker stores. The Los Angeles–based Carter Hawley Hale Stores Inc., the owner of the Broadway, Weinstock's, Emporium, Thalhimers and Neiman-Marcus stores, owned Wanamakers, the 125-year-old Philadelphia mainstay. Carter Hawley Hale was eager to sell the marginally profitable Wanamaker stores, and Taubman was interested in Wanamakers' real estate. Taubman also felt that Woodward & Lothrop and John Wanamaker were identical in size and style in their prospective markets. The combined stores created a potential $1 billion retailer, and Woodies chairman Edwin Hoffman was put in charge of merging the operations. The merger brought Hoffman back to Wanamaker's, the company that forcefully ousted him twenty years prior. Many people interpreted Hoffman's return to Wanamaker's as some form of revenge. "It seemed like a vanity purchase for Ed Hoffman," says one former Woodies employee. "It was as if he was saying, 'Now I got you again.'" But Hoffman states that that was certainly not the case. "When Al said he wanted to buy John Wanamaker, I wanted to run for the hills," says Hoffman. "It was a dog, but we got it so cheap. Al insisted that we had to buy it." Hoffman also told *Philadelphia Magazine* in April 1989, "I had absolutely no interest [in running Wanamaker's]. Life was serene—why complicate it with that?"[117] An executive from Carter Hawley Hale, Wanamakers' previous owner, agreed with that notion: "Ed Hoffman, in the twilight of his career, needed Wanamaker's like he needed a hole in the head. He took it on because he had no choice. It was just another opportunity for Al Taubman to make money."

Taubman asked Hoffman to merge Wanamaker's operations into Woodies' and not maintain two separate divisions. The valuable John Wanamaker name was kept, but most of the store's support staff was dismissed. Wanamaker's was no longer a Philadelphia operation. "It was an opportunity [for Taubman] to squeeze more profits out of both [stores]," reported *Philadelphia Magazine*.[118] Former Woodies president Robert Mang states that Wanamaker's took valuable energy away from the profitable yet vulnerable Woodward & Lothrop stores:

> *The merger with John Wanamaker was a good move geographically and in terms of image. I don't know if the merger was handled very well. Both stores were similar in that they had the same problem of having a behemoth downtown location that was costly to operate. These stores took so much of the management's focus.*

For many years, the John Wanamaker stores were in desperate need of attention. The Center City store was much too big for the sales volume it produced, but it was a sacred monument. Buyer Donald Godrey recalled the merger's struggles. "We inherited stores that had worn carpet, leaky roofs and damaged ceiling tiles. We spent a ton of money fixing up those stores."

Wanamaker's had already lost its way in the Philadelphia market, and the merger created stores that were stocked solely with merchandise geared toward Washingtonians. Philadelphians were very different department store customers than Washingtonians. Donald Godfrey elaborates, "John Wanamaker had a different clientele than Woodies. It was more of a blue-collar store. The customers in Philadelphia were experts in big-time sales. If the sale price wasn't more than 50 percent off, then they'd just think about it."

The merger completely taxed the company's resources. "The combination of Woodward & Lothrop and John Wanamaker never got off the ground because the company didn't have the money to invest or compete," says executive vice-president Howard Lehrer. Within a few months of the Wanamaker purchase, Taubman filed suit with Carter Hawley Hale. He stated that Wanamakers' value had been misrepresented and that he had been overcharged by more than $50 million. In August 1987, the two parties settled their dispute. The details of the agreement were not disclosed, but

Carter Hawley Hale acknowledged that a "minor adjustment" was made to the final purchase price.

The combination of the two stores created stress and strain at Woodward & Lothrop's corporate offices. President Robert Mang explains, "Mergers and acquisitions are a management distraction. Every department store has about one hundred buyers, and they take on a lot of extra workload. It doesn't always work so well." The two stores struggled to combine their technological systems. The conflicting systems created merchandise delivery delays between the warehouse and the stores. Employee morale began to erode, and the company offered retirement incentive packages to reduce its staff force. Longtime buyer Shirley Mihursky left the company in 1988. "They offered early retirement, and I took it," says Mihursky. "The writing was on the wall, and there was this feeling that the doors were going to close." The situation worsened in 1988, when Macy's and Nordstrom opened their first Washington stores. Nordstrom posed the biggest threat to medium and upper Washington retailers. Founded in Seattle in 1901, Nordstrom was known for exemplary customer service and a massive shoe department. It was the retail industry trailblazer, and Washingtonians embraced the store's arrival. Vice-chairman Robert Mulligan recalled, "The biggest name in retailing that came to Washington was Nordstrom. It lived a darling life, and the press loved Nordstrom." As the competition intensified in the Washington market, Woodward & Lothrop remained focused on its loyal local customer base. "We didn't give up providing good customer service and staying close to the community," says former president Robert Mang. "But customers love something new."

One of the store's biggest missteps occurred at its once lucrative Tysons Corner location in Virginia. In May 1987, Woodies' newly installed president Tom L. Roach stated, "We'll be prepared [for Nordstrom's!] by the time they arrive not only in terms of fashion and quality merchandise, but [also] in selection, presentation, and the overall atmosphere of our new Tysons store." However, construction delays and funding issues delayed Woodies' renovation at Tysons. When Nordstrom celebrated its grand opening in March 1988 at Tysons Corner, the Woodward & Lothrop store was midway through the massive reconstruction. When customers flocked to Tysons to experience the new Nordstrom store, they stayed away from Woodies' immense construction zone. It was an incredible lost opportunity for the company. "While Nordstrom, Hecht's, and Macy's beckoned with fresh glitz [at Tysons in 1988], Woodies looked as if it belonged in downtown Beirut," said retail analyst Kenneth Gassman.[119] Sales at the Tysons Woodward &

The popular and profitable Tysons Corner location received significant competition from Nordstrom, Bloomingdale's and a reinvigorated Hecht's store. *Photograph by the author.*

Woodward & Lothrop unfortunately timed its renovation at Tysons Corner to coincide with the opening of the area's first Nordstrom. Many design features of the downtown store were incorporated into the Tysons store but the lengthy renovation eroded company sales figures. *Photograph by the author.*

Lothrop store dropped 70 percent during the construction. Chairman Edwin Hoffman bemoaned, "[Woodies] never lost market share…until we began to tear the Tysons Corner store apart."[120] In September 1988, reports surfaced that Al Taubman was interested in selling the department store. Woodies was not officially for sale, but Taubman solicited interest and advice for his stores. Economically, it was a terrible time to sell a department store company. The retail world was struggling from sluggish sales and was exhausted from numerous mergers and takeovers. The once mighty Woodward & Lothrop stores attracted few offers and appeared in a state of crisis. A controversial article appeared in the *Regardie's* magazine publication. *Regardie's* was a hard-hitting local periodical that ceased publication in 1992 due to declining advertising revenue. The 1988 article titled "What the hell happened to Woodies?" exposed problems at the department store and laid blame on Al Taubman and the store's chairman, Ed Hoffman. The article read:

> *The boys in Detroit* [Taubman] *wanted to save some dough pronto… Taubman wanted Hoffman to merge* [Woodies and Wanamaker's] *so he could squeeze out more profits…All* [Hoffman] *wants to do is fill out the rest of his contract, which is up in September* [1989] *and go quietly to his home next to a golf course in Florida….Nordstrom has fantastic service. Macy's is the new glitzy guy on the block. Hecht's has everything that I need. Why Woodies? What makes it special? It's hard to say. Somewhere along the line it gave up its identity…What the hell happened to Woodies? How did a stable, family-run company become a pawn on the national takeover chessboard? The answers are unsettling.*

The magazine called Hoffman "a yesterday kind of merchant and 20 years behind the times as a merchandiser." The article became a Washington sensation and infuriated Hoffman. He pulled Woodies' advertisements from *Regardie's* right before the important Christmas selling season. Ed Hoffman looks back at the article, calling it a "sore spot." He insists, "Nobody gave much credibility to Bill Regardie. He was a prick." In the long run, the article didn't matter. By February 1989, Taubman decided to keep Woodies, along with its sister Wanamaker stores. Taubman decided to invest more money into the business and change company leadership. Ed Hoffman stepped down and Arnold Aaronson became the new chairman. The February 1989 issue of the in-store newsletter, the *Woodlothian*, included a farewell message from Ed Hoffman that included his defense of the company's sale to Taubman:

The once mighty art deco Silver Spring Hecht Company ended its run in 1987. It is now the home of the City Place Mall. *Courtesy of the Richard Longstreth Collection.*

The Board of Directors and I were convinced there would be an unfriendly takeover of Woodies if we didn't do something to protect our future. The decision was made to sell to the Taubman Company. I believed then, and I believe now, this was the finest decision I made during my 41-year career in retailing…It's not easy to end one's working days and embark on a new life, but I do so with no regrets. God bless you all.

After being named chairman, Aaronson noted, "We want Woodies to have the right style rather than just be trendy and avant-garde, it's the difference between style and stylish." Unable to secure a suitable offer for the department store group, Taubman took Woodward & Lothrop's off the sales market. Taubman said he would increase his financial commitment to the stores and focus on Woodies' long-term success. "Taubman was known for buying something, keeping it for a few years, and flipping it," says a former Woodward & Lothrop employee. "Taubman had no choice but to keep it [because there were no offers.]"

By the time Aaronson arrived in 1989, the country was in a recession. The stores were reportedly still making money, but annual sales and profits continued to fall. The *Washington Times* cited three mistakes that the company made that further hurt the organization:

> •*Woodward & Lothrop expanded its home furnishings business and opened two specialty furniture stores, despite the country's economic troubles.*
> •*Woodies invested $50 million into the Center City Philadelphia John Wanamaker store, reducing its size and prominence. Even though Taubman earned money from the building's sale* [Wanamaker's Center City store was sold in 1987, and the bottom five floors were leased back to Woodies the following March] *and some of its assets, downtown department stores struggled to maintain sales and the money could have been better invested in updating Wanamaker's dowdy and neglected suburban locations.*
> •*Woodies continued to upgrade its high-quality clothing lines* [such as] *DKNY and Ellen Tracey while many of its counterparts focused on more moderate lines to buoy sales during the economic slump.*[121]

Critics warned that the store's commitment to slower moving merchandise offerings could destroy the company's finances. "The top-quality stores have taken the cream out of the marketplace, and Woodies is left to slug it out for the leftovers," said one retail expert.

Washington retailing suffered a significant psychological blow when Garfinckel's announced its bankruptcy and liquidation on June 21, 1990. Garfinckel's was the victim of multiple ownership changes and varying shopping patterns. "Garfinckel's was clearly a victim of corporate raiding by those who cleaned out all of its assets," says historian John DeFerrari. Garfinckel's lost its place. There was a time when Garfinckel's was the pinnacle of Washington fashion, a store "that traded a step above Woodward & Lothrop and had a certain snob appeal." Shoppers and residents mourned the store's closure although many of its customers had abandoned it in favor of Neiman-Marcus, Saks Fifth Avenue and other out-of-town merchants. News reports of Garfinckel's closing read "like an obituary of your family's most elegant older friend." Woodies president Arnold Aaronson lamented, "We are shocked and saddened by the closing of Garfinckel's. No one can deny that these are perilous times for retailers in general. At the same time, we [Woodies] are convinced that we are on the right track." The *Washington Post* asked, "Where will we go to ask about

The Iverson Mall Woodward & Lothrop was strategically merchandised for its surrounding customer base in Prince George's County. *Photograph by the author.*

linen sheets, the care of pearls, the size of tea napkins and how many inches a cloth should hang over the dining table?"[122]

By the end of 1991, Hecht's claimed the title of Washington's top-grossing department store. Hecht's continually strengthened its performance in its Washington and Baltimore stores and expanded its presence in Virginia and North Carolina by merging with Thalhimers in Richmond, Virginia. Hecht's succeeded by "quietly plugging along with its middle-of-the-road offerings, competent presentation, very little debt, and solid management."[123] While Hecht's increased its market share, Al Taubman increased his personal subsidy of Woodward & Lothrop in order to avoid a financial disaster. Once the hometown favorite, Woodies fought for survival. President Arnold Aaronson blamed the costly Persian Gulf War for some of the company's missed sales goals. He felt that customers were uncertain about their economic situations and were making only necessary purchases.[124] He asked employees at Woodies and Wanamaker's to redouble their "creativity, energy, and hard work in order to get through this difficult period."[125] Taubman lost patience with the store's performance. The company floundered as its merchandise changes confused loyal customers. Its Philadelphia John Wanamaker stores competed with Macy's and a weakening Strawbridge & Clothier. Woodies

The interior of the Iverson store was more simple and modest in design than the other Woodward & Lothrop branch locations. *Photograph by the author.*

Landover Mall became one of the Washington area's most challenging shopping centers. Once a powerful retail center, Landover struggled from the gradual loss of tenants and the perception of poor safety in the area. *Photograph by the author.*

An interior photograph of the quiet Landover Mall Woodies store shortly before its closing sale in 1995. *Photograph by the author.*

recommitted its efforts to be a dominant, full-line department store company that was differentiated by exemplary service and merchandise that was "perceptibly unique." The effort was not enough to stem the losses. Former executive vice-president Howard Lehrer says, "Woodward & Lothrop could have succeeded longer than it did without the merger with John Wanamaker. But Woodies would have had to eventually merge with another retailer [in order to survive]."

Everybody Wants Woodies to Survive

By 1993, Woodies was drowning in debt and rumors circulated that Woodward & Lothrop was contemplating a Chapter 11 bankruptcy filing. Alfred Taubman was impatient with the department store's performance and spent another $262 million to keep the company afloat. Management denied the bankruptcy speculation, but a January 1994 article in the *Women's Wear Daily* trade publication reported that although Woodies had no plans for a bankruptcy filing, the department store was always aware of its "alternatives." The *Washington Post* stated, "a bankruptcy filing would be a serious blow to Woodies' reputation, and plunge it into a costly and prolonged legal battle."[126] Just three days later, Woodward & Lothrop filed for Chapter 11 bankruptcy protection. On February 2, 1994, the company stated in its *Woodlothian* newsletter, "The amount of debt and interest we have carried for the past several years makes our balance sheet weak, and this fact interferes with our ability to compete effectively." Around 10,500 workers worried about their employment future even though Woodies promised that business would continue as usual.

President Robert Mang says, "[Woodward & Lothrop's] bankruptcy was more of a balance sheet problem than an operating problem, but the company did not have enough cash flow to pay off [the debt's] high interest rates. Chapter 11 is really a tool where you can come out with a healthier balance sheet." A creditor's committee was formed to oversee the department store's reorganization, and vendors lined up to show their support for the company. The Mid-Atlantic chapter of the United Food and Commercial

Under the artistic direction of Michael Graves, the downtown Woodward & Lothrop store enjoyed a major design renovation in 1986. The renovation created excitement, but its sales resurgence was somewhat short lived. *Photograph by the author.*

Workers praised management's long-term commitment to the department store, and Estee Lauder Inc. said that, even though they were owed $603,000 in past bills, the cosmetics firm was "sticking by [Woodies] through thick and thin." Even Gary H. Bugge, the court-appointed chairman of the creditor's committee, acknowledged that "everybody wants Woodies to survive."[127] The bankruptcy resulted in casualties. After five decades of operation, the store's small Pentagon branch closed in May 1994. The 8,200-square-foot store, an early Palais Royal branch, suffered from declining sales due to a decrease in the Pentagon's workforce. The company hired a new president and chief operating officer, Edwin J. Holman, who indicated a need to streamline the company's sales and executive staff. Store leadership regretfully canceled the traditional Twenty Year Club celebratory banquet as the company felt that it was "not appropriate for [Woodward & Lothrop] to be spending thousands of dollars entertaining large numbers of our people during our reorganization process." This announcement appeared in the company's *Woodlothian* in-store newsletter, which ceased publication in May 1994.

In September 1994, Woodward & Lothrop executives presented a five-year restructuring plan to the court-designated creditor's committee. The plan included the elimination of several middle-management jobs combined with updated advertising and merchandising strategies. However, disappointing sales during the Christmas 1994 season thwarted the company's immediate turnaround strategy. Back in 1994, Woodies president Robert Mang recruited Howard Lehrer, a thirty-year retail veteran, to assist the department store with its recovery. Lehrer says, "The [entire Washington] community and the manufacturing community was hoping Woodies would survive. But it was too far gone. We had the funds to fill the stores [with merchandise] but it was a difficult environment to reorganize. It wasn't financially feasible to continue [in business]." Buyer and store director Donald Godfrey agrees with this assessment: "Each of the stores made money, but you can't survive when you are paying a debt load with 14 percent interest; no company can." Woodward & Lothrop revaluated all of its stores in terms of sales potential. "The Annapolis store was pretty questionable, and Landmark was not doing well," says Lehrer. On March 17, 1995, Woodies announced the closure of two of its three stores in Prince George's County, Maryland, along with its once successful branch at Seven Corners in Falls Church, Virginia. Seven Corners offered little growth potential in a market that experienced a dramatic demographic transition. The Prince George's County locations, at Landover Mall and Prince George's Plaza, were among the chain's least profitable stores. It was a blow to the county as Prince George's suffered with its image as a community known for "economic and racial struggles."[128] Former chairman Edwin Hoffman reflected, "The Prince George's County stores didn't do well. It wasn't quite our territory." The company also liquidated its far-flung Wanamaker's branch in Yonkers, New York. Woodies wanted to concentrate its remaining available resources on its more productive locations but that proved difficult.

Upon its initial bankruptcy filing, Woodward & Lothrop promised a quick reorganization, but as the process lingered into its second year, the future seemed pessimistic. "Throughout most of the two-year process, employee morale was good," says executive vice-president Howard Lehrer. "But anger soon developed because people had built their careers by being focused on one organization." Store director Donald Godfrey expands that idea: "Everybody felt the brunt of the bankruptcy. There was a shroud hanging over the store. Everybody from buyers to warehouse workers to customers knew that we were going to go out of business." Godfrey was correct. Credits and vendors lost faith in the store's recovery. "[Chairman] Bob Mang was moving the company in the best direction that he could," says a former Woodward & Lothrop

The aging Seven Corners Woodward & Lothrop store, as seen in 1994, was maintained but lacked sufficient sales growth. *Photograph by the author.*

The Wheaton location remained popular with its loyal local customer base. *Courtesy of the Richard Longstreth Collection.*

executive. However, by spring 1995, Mang realized that the future of the company was bleak. "The creditor committee felt that our real estate value was in excess of our business as an outgoing concern," recalled Mang. Rumors surfaced that Federated Department Stores and Dillard Department Stores were interested in making an offer for the bankrupt organization. Even Local 400 of the United Food and Commercial Workers Union explored its own buyout plan in order to preserve the nearly six thousand union employers at Woodies' Washington stores. "It's a credit that we were viewed as a viable competitor," says Mang.

In early June 1995, Federated Department Stores, the operator of Washington's three Macy's stores and two Bloomingdale's locations, made a formal offer to Woodward & Lothrop. Federated agreed to purchase "a minimum of eleven Woodward & Lothrop stores" and convert the locations to the Macy's nameplate.[129] The purchase required bankruptcy court approval and did not include the downtown Washington store. "We started the month [June 1995] with Federated making a tentative offer," says chairman Robert Mang. "We talked to the creditor committee who felt that we didn't have to think very hard [to accept the offer]." The Woodies purchase was the perfect vehicle for Federated to expand its Washington presence. The Philadelphia John Wanamaker stores would be divided between three buyers: Strawbridge & Clothier, Boscov's and the Rubin Organization, a retail shopping center developer. Customers greeted the news with sadness but were not surprised by the company's decision. Some shoppers viewed the sale in a positive light since Woodies had lost its competitive edge. In a *Washington Post* article, former chairman Edwin Hoffman expressed his sentiment on the store's demise:

> *I'm sorry, but not surprised. It was a very nice, somewhat slow-moving, genteel, fine Southern department store. It was a nicely managed store in an economy that wasn't really red hot. [But] the store was not aggressive. We just did business every day.*[130]

In another *Post* article entitled "Once There Was a Woodies," a number of Washingtonians reminisced about their former favorite store:

> *Farewell, Woodies. Farewell to the days of the downtown department store, where ladies put on hats and gloves to shop for sheets. Farewell to the annual trip to see the Christmas windows and shudder in delicious anticipation on Santa's lap. Farewell to Easter dresses, tea sandwiches, and the notions*

counter…When I first moved here in 1982, I favored Bloomingdales. I was chastised by a friend from law school—a native Washingtonian—who told me that since I lived here, I ought to shop at Woodies. Because that was the store for Washington…Shopping at Woodies was a sign that you'd made it…It represented a lifestyle and attitude that you wanted to reach: "Wouldn't it be nice if you could afford to shop regularly at Woodies? Woodies was like marrying a dentist"…Woodies was like the beautiful cheerleader who never changed. It got, well, too dowdy.[131]

Federated planned to convert its purchased Woodward & Lothrop stores by the upcoming Christmas selling season. The remaining unsold Woodies stores in Washington would be liquidated.

However, the announced purchase agreement quickly became complicated. "As soon as we announced the deal [to Federated], the May Company wanted to get into the game," says chairman Robert Mang. "They didn't want Macy's to be the powerhouse in Washington." May Department Stores was the owner of Hecht's, Washington's dominant department store company. May wanted to purchase the Philadelphia Wanamaker stores and team up with J.C. Penney Co. for the Washington stores. May planned to convert the Philadelphia John Wanamaker stores into the Hecht's nameplate. The change was a psychological blow to Philadelphia, a city known for its strong traditions. Some Woodward & Lothrop stores, such as Tysons Corner and Wheaton Plaza, would become J.C. Penney stores, and others, such as Landmark and Lake Forest, would become Lord & Taylor, a May owned division. The downtown flagship Woodies was not a part of May's offer. However, "Chevy Chase was a great

After 115 years together, we have one final thing to say…

Thank you.

Our historic liquidation sale begins tomorrow morning at 8am sharp.

WOODWARD & LOTHROP

Woodies' final advertisement, thanking its customers for 115 years of loyalty, appeared on August 31, 1995. *Collection of the author.*

store," recalls Mang. "It was the only store in Washington that May wanted to operate as a Hecht's." On August 8, 1995, May Department Stores, along with J.C. Penney, won the bid for Woodies' assets after a fierce bidding war. The biding war was a "stealth attack" to limit Federated's presence in Washington. The May-Penney agreement fetched $590 million for the company compared to Federated's $439 million offer.[132] It formally marked the end of the line for Woodward & Lothrop and John Wanamaker stores.

The end of Woodward & Lothrop was especially difficult for its loyal group of executives and support staff. "[Woodies' employees] were special people who took great pride in the store," says former vice-president David Mullen. "They worked to make the store a success." Chairman Robert Mang recalls the store's final days:

> *It was the loss of an iconic store. People cried; employees cried. But we saved rank and file jobs* [by selling to May-Penney]. *The higher-level jobs didn't survive. The people who* [financially] *invested in the store walked out with a nice return. We were able to sell the company. I remember the final ad. There were lots of tears…Retailing gets in your blood, and blood gets into your heart. You become a shopkeeper at heart. Retailing never gets out of your blood.*

On September 1, 1995, Woodward & Lothrop began its liquidation sale. The retail liquidation firm, Gordon Brothers, purchased Woodies' inventory for approximately $100 million and conducted the closeout. Crowds formed at all Woodward & Lothrop locations, except Chevy Chase, and were promised historic savings. Customers were outraged at the paltry markdowns and felt betrayed by the promises of a "historic" sale. A spokesperson for the liquidator, Gordon Brothers, said, "Disgruntled bargain hunters vote with their pocketbooks, and history has shown they will return when further markdowns are made in another week or two." As the liquidation sale continued, the discount grew from 10 percent off in its initial week to 90 percent off in its final hours. Woodies "vanished into history" on November 10, 1995. Although they received a slightly lower return on the merchandise for the final sale, Gordon Brothers decorated Woodies' downtown flagship store for a final early Christmas season as a present to longtime Washingtonians.

As J.C. Penney Co. prepared to convert its seven acquired Woodies locations for a July 1996 opening, the former downtown Woodward & Lothrop flagship awaited its future. On January 23, 1996, arts patron and socialite Betty Brown Casey announced her plans to purchase the downtown Woodies as a new home for the Washington Opera. Her late husband, Eugene Casey, was a former agricultural advisor to President Franklin D. Roosevelt and was described by the *Washington Post* as a "former Maryland politician, racetrack owner, and prison inmate."[133] In 1946, Eugene Casey had spent five months in prison for federal tax evasion. Opera supporters applauded the announcement and move since the Washington Opera did not receive the same level of commitment at its Kennedy Center home as the National Symphony Orchestra. However, the plan baffled many downtown leaders. Woodies' exterior was protected with historical designation and the D.C. Zoning Commission dictated that 50 percent of the building must be used for retail purposes. The *Post* observed, "Exactly what the [Washington Opera] company is going to *do* with the building remains to be seen."[134] Initial plans called for the interior of the former department store to be removed and rebuilt as an opera house. "It was a ridiculous proposal to stick an opera house in that building," says architectural historian and Georgetown University professor Richard Longstreth. "Even a person in charge of implanting the design approached [the D.C. review committee] said, 'Please tell me that this proposal is a pile of crap.'" In addition, Longstreth says that opera houses do not generate business like museums, and it would have been a "deadening factor" for that immediate downtown area: "Downtown still needed a lot of oomph." After learning that the conversion to an opera house would cost over $200 million, Casey sold the building to developer Douglas Jemal in February 1999. Jemal and his company, Douglas Development Corporation, tried to find tenants for the former Woodies flagship but were unsuccessful. For over a year, Jemal courted Macy's to fill the building's bottom three floors. Rumors abounded that Lord & Taylor and Wal-Mart were interested in the building. In 2003, Jemal received his first break when Swedish clothier H&M became the first of several tenants to occupy the building's lower floors. Although portions of its ornate exterior have been painted garishly, the Douglas Development Corporation has transformed the former Woodward & Lothrop into the home of such businesses as the General Services Administration, the National Endowment for Democracy, the Recording Industry Association and the Pew Charitable Trusts, along with H&M, Zara, Forever 21 and Madame Tussauds Museum. It has brought new life to the Washington fixture. "At least it's up and running," says Longstreth. "It was lying fallow for a number of years. I think that [its redevelopment] is for the better. You can always remove paint."

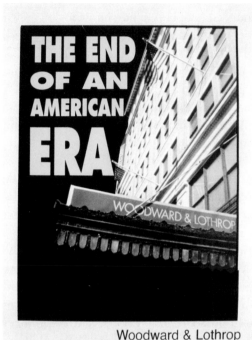

Woodward & Lothrop

Instead of loud blaring closing signs, the Gordon Brothers firm chose more sedate and tasteful signs for the liquidation sales. However, the initial sales discounts angered and insulted many shoppers. *Collection of the author.*

The late Rutgers University professor and historian Charles F. Cummings summed up the department store experience in a 2002 essay published in the *Newark Star-Ledger*:

> *Big downtown stores were the hubs of major shopping centers. It was a time when your aunt, mother, or grandmother brought you to town to shop in the stores, eat in the many restaurants and go to a matinee before heading home for supper. This was the age of the shopping temple: floorwalkers, banks of elevators, seasonal displays of merchandise, store restaurants, scores of attentive clerks, a general policy that the customer is always right and the willingness to exchange merchandise if the customer was not pleased with a purchase.*[135]

Although Cummings's comments referred to the big Newark, New Jersey department stores, his sentiment is applicable to most of America's grand emporiums. These stores provided merchandise, entertainment, meals, employment and social opportunities for generations of customers. For 115 years, no Washington department store did this "better" than Woodies. Woodward & Lothrop rightfully earned its title, "A Store Worthy of the Nation's Capital."

Seventh-Floor Tea

THE WOODIES TEA ROOM

Jan Whitaker

Opened around 1921, the tearoom in Woodward & Lothrop attracted slow-moving lines of hungry but patient diners right up to the time the store closed in 1995. Despite the exodus of so many customers to the suburbs after World War II, people still rode up to the seventh floor, through better and worse, to lunch on chicken pot pies, apple Betty and, later, salads from the Express Buffet.

Duncan Hines's "Adventures in Good Eating" praised Woodies' tearoom in 1947 for its deviled crab and classic Wellesley fudge cake. At that time, children enjoyed their own dining room, "popular with mothers and little children." Hard to believe, but the Children's Room Mother Goose Luncheon menu of the 1950s offered dishes, such as a plate of vegetables or a poached egg in a nest of spinach, that would scarcely appeal to children today. Those with very light appetites could settle for a bowl of crackers and milk.

In the mid-twentieth century, the tearoom was known for its excellent food at reasonable prices, and it ranked with other above-average department store restaurants, such as Joseph Horne in Pittsburgh and Meier & Frank in Portland, Oregon. The store advertised it as a place that would "appeal to those who prefer to lunch without too much diversion." Afternoon tea was

The store's signature seventh-floor Tea Room operated as the Terrace Room during its final years. *Photograph by the author.*

In the 1950s, Woodward & Lothrop operated a children-only Tea Room on its seventh floor. *Collection of the author.*

served by candlelight from 2:30 p.m. to 5:30 p.m. in the adjoining Little Tea Room. As befit a quietly refined department store's tearoom, no liquor was served. To the dismay of some, that would change.

A 1951 menu describes quintessential tearoom dishes, such as fruit salad plates with orange cottage cheese, and other, more piquant selections, such as "Crab Ravigote, Tomato Aspic, Deviled Egg, Cress, Potato Salad, A Roll," all for $1.25 (about $11.00 today). Classic sandwiches that shout "department store cuisine" were cream cheese and nut on cinnamon raisin bread with pineapple cherry preserves ($0.45) and grilled mushroom, cress and bacon on white bread with pickles ($0.55). Where could you find a menu today with such gems as chilled prune juice (an appetizer), chicken-filled biscuits or frozen almond ball with bittersweet sauce? If guests didn't want a pot of tea ($0.15), they could order a glass of buttermilk.

The 1950s were mostly a golden era for department stores, Woodies included. But then things got tougher. Old-time customers scattered, rarely shopping downtown. Younger customers stayed away, attracted neither to the store's fashions nor to its tearoom. In the 1970s, though, it was still possible to lure "career girls" working downtown with a buffet and fashion show designed for them, for admission of only three dollars. But the wish to attract free-spending teens meant that the store's mid-1970s remodeling would do away with the downstairs budget store, replacing it with youth shops and a food court cleverly named EatCetera.

After the major renovation of the mid-1980s, the tearoom had to compete with additional restaurants beyond EatCetera and the downstairs cafeteria, once known as the Fountain Room, renamed Counter Culture. On the seventh floor, next to the tearoom was the Saratoga Buffet Company with its lengthy salad bar, while on the second-floor men's section was the English Pub.

But still, customers came to the tearoom, perhaps for its homey chicken pot pie and sweet potato pie. A critic complained that the four-hundred-seat interior was "plain jane" and did not seem to have been touched in the expensive renovation campaign. And it's true that features such as gumwood paneling, thick columns and draperies would seem dull to younger diners used to colorful chain restaurants. It's likely that eating there then was either a sentimental journey or simply a convenience for those working nearby who wanted a quick salad from the salad bar.

By the early 1990s, perhaps before, the tearoom was renamed Terrace Restaurant and supplied with an updated menu reflecting the nation's turn toward ethnic dishes, such as Thai Shrimp. Chicken pot pie could still be had, but in many respects, the restaurant was running on empty. A customer, visiting the old tearoom after an absence of almost forty years, expressed regret when she discovered the tearoom had been transformed: "It was a restaurant with things like roast beef dinners with gravy instead of chicken salad sandwiches, and martinis instead of tea, and forget about hot fudge."

Actually, as far back as the 1950s, the tearoom served hearty dishes, such as fried chicken and bean soup. But still, in a true sense, Woodward & Lothrop's tearoom was gone, a victim of the times, residing only in memory.

Jan Whitaker is an internationally known department store expert and historian. She is the author of several books including *Tea at the Blue Lantern Inn: A Social History of the Tea Room Craze in America*, *The World of Department Stores* and *Service and Style: How the American Department Store Fashioned the Middle Class*.

"DAINTY TASTY" TEA SANDWICHES

Deviled Crab

Combine 1 cup crabmeat and ¾ cup chopped celery. Moisten mixture with mayonnaise. Spread a layer of mayonnaise on two slices of brown bread. Place a helping of crabmeat on one half of bread and place a tomato slice on the other. Garnish with watercress and press two halves together. Remove crust and cut into triangles.

Egg Salad

Separate the whites and yolks from six hard-boiled eggs. Mash the yolks and press them through a sieve. Finely chop the egg whites. Mix the egg yolks and egg whites and season with salt, pepper and paprika. Add a small amount of chopped sweet pickles. Moisten mixture with mayonnaise. Spread a layer of mayonnaise on two slices of thin white bread. Place a small amount of egg on both halves of bread and press two halves together. Remove crust and cut into triangles.

Wellesley Fudge Cupcakes

CAKE:

4 squares Baker's unsweetened
  chocolate
½ cup water
1¾ cups sugar
1⅔ cups flour
1 teaspoon baking soda
1 teaspoon salt
½ cup butter
3 eggs
¾ cup milk
1 teaspoon vanilla

FROSTING:

4 squares Baker's unsweetened
  chocolate
2 tablespoons butter
1-pound box of powdered sugar
salt
½ cup milk
1 teaspoon vanilla

Preheat oven to 350 degrees. Prepare 24 cupcake tins with liners. Heat chocolate, water and ½ cup sugar in a small saucepan, stirring constantly for 2 minutes. Remove from heat and let cool. Meanwhile, combine flour, baking soda and salt and set aside.

Cream butter and remaining sugar together until light and fluffy. Add eggs, one at a time, beating constantly. Slowly add flour mixture alternately with milk, beating until smooth. Add vanilla and cooled chocolate and blend. Divide batter among the 24 cupcake tins. Cook for 20 to 25 minutes, until inserted toothpick comes out clean.

Make frosting by melting chocolate and butter over low heat, stirring constantly until smooth. Remove from heat and let cool. Combine sugar, salt, milk and vanilla. Add chocolate and blend well. Spread frosting generously and quickly on cooked cupcakes. Add a small amount of milk if frosting becomes too thick.

"Metro Chicken" from the Culinary Arcade

Mix skinless breasts of chicken with a generous amount of teriyaki sauce and sliced spring onions. Cover and marinate overnight. Grill chicken, without spring onions, until cooked.

FRICASSE OF CHICKEN

Cut a whole chicken into serving pieces while leaving the breasts whole. Cook chicken in boiling water seasoned with one half of a sliced onion, three peppercorns and a bay leaf. Cook slowly for 1 to 1½ hours, or until tender, and add 2 teaspoons of salt halfway through the cooking. Remove from water and set aside. Keep chicken warm while making sauce.

Make the sauce by reducing the stock in the pot and strain. Melt 4 tablespoons of butter in the stock pot and add 4 tablespoons of flour, stirring constantly. Gradually, add the chicken stock and bring the mixture to a boil. Season with salt and pepper. Add 1 cup of sliced sautéed mushrooms.

Place serving of chicken on top of steamed rice and cover with sauce.

ℕotes

Boston Store

1. F.E. Woodward, "Experiences of the Founders Before Coming to Washington," *Woodlothian* magazine (December 24, 1924).
2. Martha C. Guilford, *From Founders to Grandsons: The Story of Woodward & Lothrop* (Washington, D.C.: Rufus H. Darby, 1955), 24.
3. Woodward, "Experiences."
4. Bernard McDonnell, "The Boston House Grew Great from 'One Price' Start," *Washington Post*, October 4, 1925.

"Alvin, This Is the Place for Us"

5. Robert E.L. Johnson, *Woodward & Lothrop: Portrait of a Corporate Institution* (Washington, D.C.: Woodward & Lothrop, 1964), 12.
6. Company advertisement, *Washington Post*, February 25, 1980.
7. Guilford, *From Founders to Grandsons*, 43.
8. McDonnell, "Boston House."
9. *Washington Post*, "Woodward & Lothrop's New Store: A Business Palace," April 2, 1887.
10. Johnson, *Woodward & Lothrop*, 12.
11. Company advertisement, *Baltimore Sun*, March 15, 1893.

12. *Washington Post*, "Treasures in a Wigwam," December 7, 1897.

13. Ibid., "At Woodward & Lothrop's: A Millinery Opening That Will Attract All Feminine Washington," March 3, 1903.

14. Jan Whitaker, *Service and Style: How the American Department Store Fashioned the Middle Class* (New York: St. Martin's Press, 2006).

15. *Washington Post*, "Church Thronged at Funeral of Washington Merchant," December 3, 1912.

16. Ibid., "S. Walter Woodward, Prominent Merchant of Washington Dies Unexpectedly at Summer Home," August 3, 1917.

17. Unknown author, Woodward & Lothrop company papers, Historical Society of D.C.

18. Guilford, *Founders to Grandsons*, 191.

19. John Tyssowski, "As I See It," *Woodlothian* magazine (June 1956).

20. George Porter, "Exceptional Chorus Organized in Local Store," *Washington Post*, February 14, 1926.

THE POSSIBLE YEARS

21. Richard Longstreth, *The American Department Store Transformed, 1920–1960* (New Haven, CT: Yale University Press, 2010), 33.

22. "An Emerging Major Retailer," Woodward & Lothrop Annual Report, 1980.

23. Longstreth, *American Department Store Transformed*, 76.

24. "*House & Garden* Honors Colonial Williamsburg," company advertisement, October 28, 1937.

NORTH BUILDING

25. *Washington Post*, "You Are Respectfully Invited to the Opening of the New Palais Royal," October 1, 1893.

26. Ibid., "A. Lisner's New Store," January 2, 1887.

27. *Washington City Paper*, "The Day They Knocked Down the Palais Royal," May 1987.

28. Joel Sayre, "Mike Todd and His Big Bug-Eye Illusion," *Life* magazine (March 1955).

29. Guilford, *From Founders to Grandsons*, 158–9.

30. Paul Simpson, "Parker Guided Postwar Expansion of Woodie's," *Washington Post*, January 1, 1956.

31. Guilford, *From Founders to Grandsons*, 169.

32. Marion Holland, "Old-Timers Don't Say 'Woodies,'" letter to the editor, *Washington Post*, September 11, 1984.

WASHINGTON SHOPPING PLATE

33. Jack Jones, "Garfinckel's Celebrates 50th Anniversary Today," *Washington Star*, October 2, 1955.

34. *Washington Post*, "Garfinckel's Store to Open Tomorrow," October 5, 1930.

35. "We Welcome Julius Garfinckel to their Spring Valley Store," *League of Wesley Heights* magazine (August 1942).

36. Williams H. Jones, "Expansive Garfinckel to Acquire Harris," *Washington Post*, January 31, 1971.

37. *Washington Post*, "Hecht & Co. Informal Opening," March 21, 1896.

38. Richard Longstreth, "The Mixed Blessings of Success: The Hecht Company and Department Store Branch Development after World War II," *Perspectives in Vernacular Architecture* 6 (1997), 245–6.

39. Tom Burke, "Hecht Company to Mark 60 Years of Growth from Modest Beginning," *Washington Star*, March 25, 1956.

40. Longstreth, "Mixed Blessings," 247.

41. Ibid., 249.

42. *Washington Post*, "Hecht Co. Launches New Shopping Center in Arlington County," November 3, 1951.

43. Longstreth, "Mixed Blessings," 254.

44. Ibid., 256.

45. Bernard McDonnell, "Romances of Washington Stores," *Washington Post*, October 11, 1925.

46. S. Oliver Goodman, "96-Year-Old Lansburgh's Reborn Under 'Mr. Ralph,'" ibid., January 29, 1956.

47. Bailey Morris, "Adding Life to Lansburgh's," *Washington Star*, June 11, 1972.

48. Donald Baker, "As D.C.'s Oldest Department Store Prepares to Close," *Washington Post*, April 29, 1973.

49. William H. Jones, "Springfield Mall Unit Key for Lansburgh's," ibid., March 2, 1973.

50. *Washington Post*, "Things You May Expect of Kann's Virginia," November 8, 1951.

51. Larry Weekley, "1965 Prospects Bright, D.C. Retailers Say," *Washington Post,* January 10, 1965.

52. William H. Jones, Claudia Levy, "Kann's Closing Its Two Area Stores," ibid., May 22, 1975.

MARCH TO THE BELTWAY

53. Longstreth, *American Department Store Transformed*, 140.

54. Richard Longstreth, *City Center to Regional Mall*, (Cambridge, MA: MIT Press, 1997), 250.

55. Dorothea Andrews, "Growth of Suburbs Snarls D.C. Traffic," *Washington Post,* June 20, 1948.

56. Guilford, *From Founders to Grandsons*, 186.

57. *Washington Times-Herald*, "Woody's New Store Opens to Big Crowd," November 3, 1950.

58. Lucia Brown, "Woodward and Lothrop Families Help Open New Store," *Washington Post*, November 29, 1952.

59. *Washington Star*, "Fire Ruins Woody's Bethesda Store," December 17, 1954.

60. Samuel Feinberg, *What Makes Shopping Centers Tick*, (New York: Fairchild Publications, 1960), 71.

61. Jack Eisen, "7 Corners Shopping Center Open for Business Thursday," *Washington Post*, October 3, 1956.

62. S. Oliver Goodman, "Woodies List More New Store Details," ibid., September 12, 1958.

63. *Washington Post*, "Monday to Mark Formal Opening of Landmark Shopping Center," October 10, 1965.

64. S. Oliver Goodman, "McLachlen Plans New Main Office," *Washington Post*, October 11, 1963.

65. George Lardner Jr., "Woodie's Plan to Span G Street Poses Dilemma for D.C. Officials," ibid., April 14, 1965.

66. *Washington Star*, "Hecht, Woodward Plan Tyson's Corner Stores," June 13, 1965.

THE SENTIMENTAL FAVORITE

67. Whitaker, *Service and Style*, 5.

68. Longstreth, *American Department Store Transformed*, 8.

69. William L. Bird Jr., *Holidays on Display*, (New York: Princeton Architectural Press, 2007), 129.

70. *Washington Post*, "The Story of Cinderella," December 1, 1989.

71. Ibid., "Santa Claus, Arriving by Plane, Greeted with Appropriate Acclaim by Younger Set," November 12, 1950.

72. Louise Gephart, "She Sings for Her Supper," *Washington Post*, September 23, 1956.

73. *Washington Star*, "Watercolors by Hitler Attract Attention Here," November 7, 1956.

74. Longstreth, *American Department Store Transformed*, 45.

75. "Come Consult Woodward & Lothrop's Expert Wedding Service," company advertisement, January 26, 1958.

76. Roxanne Roberts, "Once There Was a Woodies," *Washington Post*, June 23, 1995.

THE "DISTURBANCE"

77. *Baltimore Afro-American*, "Department Store Discharges Girls," December 12, 1919.

78. Ibid., "Lollipop's Letter," October 22, 1927.

79. *Washington Afro-American*, "Woodward & Lothrop Is a Nice Place to Work, But—," May 19, 1956.

80. Ibid., "Woodward & Lothrop Vice Prexy Says Store Has 'Right To,'" May 26, 1956.

81. Edward Peeks, "Woodward & Lothrop Maintains Segregation," *Baltimore Afro-American*, November 24, 1956.

82. Jenn Jones, "Negro Eating Ban Is Checked," *Washington Post*, August 26, 1957.

83. *Washington Times-Herald*, "Negro Clergy Urge 1-Day Buying Ban," March 24, 1958.

84. Lynn Williams, "Capital Comment," *Pittsburgh Courier*, April 8, 1961.

85. *Washington Post*, "CORE Pickets Hecht's in Dispute," February 23, 1964.

86. Preliminary damage report, National Capital Planning Committee, May 1968.

87. Frederick A. Praeger, *Ten Blocks from the White House*, (New York: Washington Post Publishing, 1968), 71.

88. Ibid., 103.

89. Preliminary damage report, 1968.

90. Praeger, *Ten Blocks*, 182.

91. Claude Koprowski, "D.C. Retail Sales Dip Following April Riots," *Washington Post*, July 12, 1968.

92. Ibid., "Crime, Renewal Lag Seen Curb to D.C. Growth," ibid., July 5, 1968.

93. *Woodlothian* magazine (Fall 1969).

94. Longstreth, *City Center to Regional Mall*, 14.

95. Donald Baker, "As D.C.'s Oldest Department Store Prepares to Close," *Washington Post*, April 29, 1973.

Exact Change

96. S. Oliver Goodman, "Woodies Plans 'Combination' with a Midwest Retail Chain," *Washington Post*, January 12, 196.

97. Ibid., "Woodies Chief Resigns, Eyes Civic Participation," ibid., August 10, 1969.

98. William H. Jones, "Hecht Goes Mod with 'Excitement,'" ibid., August 27, 1970.

99. Robert J. Samuelson, "Woodies Launches Major Renovation," ibid., September 19, 1969.

100. Woodward & Lothrop Corporate Annual Report, 1972.

101. Margaret Shapiro, "Landover Mall Merchants Struggle to Rebuild its Image," *Washington Post*, June 24, 1980.

102. Elizabeth Thalhimer Smart, *Finding Thalhimers* (Manakin-Sabot, VA: Dementi Publishing, 2010), 187–9.

103. Ron Sander, "Woodies, Hecht's; to Accept Wide Range of Credit Cards," *Washington Star*, January 20, 1976.

104. Joe Anderson, "When the Subway Puts the City Back Together," *Washington Post*, November 16, 1969.

105. Ibid.

106. Douglas R. Feaver, "Metro Brings Extra Sales to Woodies," ibid., January 27, 1978.

107. Jane Seaberry, "Back to Drawing Board; Woodies Brings Back 'O' and '&' After Customers Reject Logo Changes," *Washington Post*, May 22, 1979.

One Hundred Years Old

108. William H. Jones and Nina S. Hyde, "Woodies Starts Second Century with Optimism," *Washington Post*, February 29, 1980.

109. Ibid.

110. Caroline E. Mayer, "Department Stores Go Modern by Marketing More of Less," ibid., August 11, 1985.

111. Ibid., "Baron: Just a 'Friendly Investor' Who Wants to Own Woodies," ibid., April 30, 1984.

112. Wendy Swallow, "Historic Woodies Building Cleared for Demolition," ibid., February 2, 1985.

113. Sarah Booth Conroy, "The Look of a Classic: Hecht's New Metro Center Store Is a Smashing Addition," ibid., November 2, 1985.

114. Caroline E. Mayer, "Nordstrom Eyes Washington Area for Expansion," ibid., December 3, 1985.

115. *Washington Post*, "Tasteful, Dreft Face Lift of Downtown Woodies," October 18, 1986.

116. John DeFerrari, Streets of Washington website, November 4, 2010.

Double Trouble

117. Laurence Hooper, "What Does It Take to Ruin a Grand Old Department Store?" *Philadelphia Magazine* (April 1989).

118. Ibid.

119. Frank O'Donnell and Harry Jaffe, "What the Hell Happened to Woodies?" *Regardie's* magazine (November 1988).

120. *Washington Business*, "Ex-Chairman: Woodies Has Learned a lot," February 20, 1989.

121. Elisa Williams, "Woodward & Lothrop Struggles," *Washington Times*, June 14, 1992.

122. Sarah Booth Conroy, "Garfinckel's, Gone with the Linen," *Washington Post*, June 22, 1990.

123. Kara Swisher, "Hecht's Takes Middle of the Retail Road to the Top," ibid., November 18, 1991.

124. Interview with Aaron Aaronson, *Woodlothian* magazine (Number 1, 1991).

125. Interview with Alfred Taubman, ibid. (Summer 1990).

EVERYBODY WANTS WOODIES TO SURVIVE

126. Kristin Downey Grimsley, "Woodward & Lothrop Calls Bankruptcy Filing an 'Option,'" *Washington Post*, January 14, 1991.

127. Ibid., "The Fallout at Woodies," ibid., February 7, 1994.

128. Margart Shapiro, "Landover Mall Merchants Struggle to Rebuild Its Image," ibid., June 24, 1980.

129. Margaret Webb Pressler, "Woodward & Lothrop Agrees to Buyout; Retail Giant Would Operate Most Stores as Macy's; Name Would Vanish," ibid., June 22, 1995.

130. Caroline E. Mayer and Frank Swoboda, "Woodies: A Grande Dame Comes to Grief," ibid., January 18, 1994.

131. Roxanne Roberts, "Once There Was a Woodies," ibid., June 23, 1995.

132. Betsy Pisik, "Hecht's Owner Wins Bid for Woodies—Seven Area Stores to be J.C. Penneys," *Washington Times*, August 9, 1995.

133. Jacqueline Trescott and Ken Ringle, "Buying Woodies for a Song," *Washington Post*, January 24, 1996.

134. Tim Page, "Sing a Song of Suspense, the Opera Gets Woodies but What Happens Next?" ibid., March 21, 1996.

135. Charles F. Cummings, "Department Store Baron Kresge Invested in the City," *Newark Star-Ledger*, May 9, 2002.

About the Author

Michael Lisicky has been credited as a nationally recognized department store "historian," "lecturer," "expert," "guru," "aficionado," "junkie" and "maven," as well as a "noted chronicler of departed East Coast department stores," by a number of major newspapers and periodicals. He is the author of several bestselling books, including *Hutzler's: Where Baltimore Shops*, *Wanamaker's: Meet Me at the Eagle* and *Baltimore's Bygone Department Stores: Many Happy Returns*. His book *Gimbels Has It!* was cited as "one of the freshest reads of 2011" by National Public Radio's *Morning Edition* program. Mr. Lisicky has given lecturers at such locations as the New York Public Library, the Boston Public Library, the Historical Society of Pennsylvania and the Baltimore Book Festival. He has been featured in *Fortune* magazine, the *Philadelphia Inquirer*, the *Dallas Morning News* and *Investor's Business Daily* and on CBS's *Sunday Morning* television program. Mr. Lisicky resides in Baltimore, where he is a musician with the Baltimore Symphony Orchestra and is a master's degree candidate in museum studies at Johns Hopkins University.